CLIENT
&
AGENCY

Working Class Responses to Casework

CLIENT
&
AGENCY

JOHN E. MAYER
& NOEL TIMMS

With a foreword by
PATRICIA DANIEL

ALDINETRANSACTION
A Division of Transaction Publishers
New Brunswick (U.S.A.) and London (U.K.)

New paperback printing 2009
Copyright © 1970 by Transaction Publishers, New Brunswick, New Jersey.

Library of Congress Catalog Number: 2009025738
ISBN: 978-0-202-36342-4
Printed in the United States of America

Library of Congress Cataloging-in-Publication Data

Mayer, John E., 1921-
    Client and agency : working class responses to casework / John E. Mayer
    and Noel Timms ; with a foreword by Patricia Daniel.
        p. cm.
    Originally published: London : routledge & K. Paul, 1970.
    Includes bibliographical references and index.
    ISBN 978-0-202-36342-4
    1. Social case work. 2. Working class--Attitudes. I. Timms, Noel.
    II. Title.

HV43.M37 2009
361.3'2--dc22
                                                        2009025738

Contents

The confusion between the interest which a person himself has or takes, and the interest which a second person has or takes in him, is one of the pitfalls of parentage, teaching, religion, and all the varied forms of professed benevolence. In order to discover whether professed benevolence is really independent benevolence, ask the beneficiary rather than the benefactor

R. B. Perry
Realms of Value

Foreword

*Patricia Daniel, formerly Casework
Consultant, Family Welfare Association*

The Family Welfare Association is pleased to be associated with the publication of this study of the views of sixty-one clients about the service they received from the Association's social work staff during the first part of 1967.

The reasons for co-operating in an enquiry of this kind were threefold. First, since people are relatively free to choose to use FWA's casework service it was thought that it would be useful to know more about the circumstances and motivation which brought them to the Association rather than to any of the many other social work services in inner London. Secondly, at the time when the study was first proposed at the beginning of 1967 it was already clear that there would be a considerable development of family services in the local authority sphere and the Association would therefore need to reconsider the future of its own family casework service. It was hoped that the study might indicate the gaps it was filling or failing to fill. Thirdly, it was thought that client opinion would be immediately relevant to the staff of FWA and probably to other social workers and teachers of social work as well.

Sixty-five clients were invited to participate in the study through a letter written by the head of the Social Work Department, and only four refused. The problems which had been most frequently focused upon by FWA social workers in their treatment were marital and economic difficulties, and these two problems were also the ones most frequently concentrated upon in the agency's total caseload during the same five-month period—January to May 1967—but the study clients had a higher proportion of marital problems, 34 per cent *vs.* 19 per cent. The study sample was a predominately working class group in that four out of five of the respondents left school at fifteen or younger and only one had gone to university; also in three out of four cases the head of the household was a manual worker.

There has been a growing awareness of the importance of consumer opinion in the social services following the widespread impact of consumer groups, particularly those concerned with educational and medical services. Social work agencies have hesitated, uncertain about the researchers and their methods, and fearful of the outcome because this kind of research involves examination of the activities of social workers as perceived by their clients and this is threatening. Social workers must feel professionally secure and supported in their practice if they are to tolerate this sort of independent examination. But it is desirable that they do so because client opinion is one way of checking the effectiveness of their work. Appropriate handling of staff involvement and reactions to research in social work organizations is crucial if practitioners are subsequently to make an intelligent critical appraisal of the findings. It is also important that the agency should have confidence in the professionalism and integrity of those conducting the research. In this study the fact that both Professor Timms and Dr Mayer were already known and trusted by a number of senior staff was an important factor in the decision to give them access to clients and in the Family Welfare Association co-operating in their project.

The practice of social work requires the application of knowledge derived from a variety of sources and academic disciplines. It is frequently difficult to relate conflicting evidence and diverse theories about human behaviour for use in day-to-day work with acutely troubled and deprived people. But the opinion of clients about what they think we do—or fail to do—with, to, or for them must surely be of significance and the importance of this preliminary study lies in the fact that it demonstrates the wealth of material which can be obtained from clients themselves, and that they can be approached with suitable safeguards. It points to the need for more extensive studies of both consumers and suppliers of social work services because it raises many pertinent questions.

Patricia Daniel

Acknowledgements

This book is the result of our collaboration which began in London and continued across the Atlantic. It represents also the fusion of two perspectives—sociological (J.M.) and social work (N.T.). We have found it a fruitful venture in co-operation, and we believe it is the kind of collaboration that holds promise for the future. However, our present debt to others is considerable.

The research on which this book is based was supported by a grant from the Johnson Fund of the American Philosophical Society. We are indebted to Patricia Daniel, formerly director of the casework services of the Family Welfare Association, London, for her interest in research and for creating a climate of opinion that enabled this project to be undertaken in the agency. We are grateful to the clients who appear in this book under fictitious names and to the social workers who gave us so much of their time. Malcolm Ford, formerly of the FWA, helped to launch the study, and Gill Brown and Mary Twyman undertook most of the interviewing. Miss E. M. Deuchar helped us by making initial contacts with many of the clients and arranging the subsequent research interview. Miss Doris Jones efficiently transcribed many of our tapes.

We are especially grateful to Dr Israel Zwerling, Director of Bronx State Hospital, for enabling one of the authors (J.M.) to take time from other duties whilst the study was being completed. Dr Zwerling has created a unique research environment at the hospital—one in which investigators are encouraged to pursue studies which have relevance not just for the hospital population, but for the mental health field as a whole.

Finally, we would like to express our thanks to Professor Aaron Rosenblatt and Professor R. M. Titmuss for reading the manuscript and making several helpful suggestions. They are, of course, in no way responsible for what follows.

John E. Mayer, *New York*
Noel Timms, *London*

1

The neglected client

My husband's gambling was driving me around the bend
and I thought maybe the Welfare could help me do
something about it. But all the lady wanted to do was
talk—what was he like when he gambled, did we quarrel,
and silly things like that. She was trying to help and it
made me feel good knowing someone cared. But you can't
solve a problem by *talking* about it. Something's got to be
done!

This is the way a former client of a social work agency summarized her experience. She came to the agency in distress,
and received some relief. At the same time she was dismayed
and perplexed by the worker's approach, and in fact failed to
return after several sessions. A research project centering around
personal reactions of this kind, whether favourable or otherwise, might well seem of limited interest, of concern only to the
clients involved and to the particular agency from which help
was sought. We believe, however, that this is not the case. The
results of our particular project, as we hope to indicate in the
concluding chapter, have implications for casework services
beyond the confines of the cases we studied. We believe, moreover, that our present study should be seen within the wider
context of what might be termed client-oriented studies. This
context, demanding a whole programme of research, has
considerable implications for administrators, social work
practitioners, policy makers and research workers who are all
concerned, though in somewhat different ways, with the

maintenance and improvement of the social services. Some of the implications of this wider programme of research will be traced in this chapter, before we come in Chapter 2 to outline our own study.

The social services constitute an important feature of our social life and are rapidly expanding to meet an increasing number of social needs. More people are being recruited as social workers, and social work help of some kind is increasingly advocated for many groups, particularly the disadvantaged. Yet, despite this fact, we are profoundly ignorant about the ways in which the consumers of these services respond to the social work help that the community makes available. Admittedly, all kinds of working assumptions are used by practitioners of social work, by administrators and policy makers about the ways in which clients see their problems, why they approach certain agencies, why they behave as they do and so forth, but these assumptions have rarely been critically examined. Clearly, until we have investigated consumer opinion we cannot begin to be sure that social work resources, likely to remain in very short supply for the foreseeable future, are deployed in the most effective way possible, to say nothing of whether they are achieving the goals for which they were designed. Nor shall we have a very firm basis for improving services in the future.

How exactly might research studies of clients be useful? As we see it, they would have somewhat different functions from the point of view of the day-to-day provision of services and the perspective of long-term improvement. Accordingly, it is useful to divide the following discussion into two parts, dwelling first on the provision of services, turning later to their improvement.

The provision of services

It seems self-evident that if administrators and policy makers are to deploy existing social work resources effectively, they will need to know at least something about the responses and reactions of those they are trying to help, specifically the manner in which the services offered are appraised. We do not mean by this that client appraisals will be, or ought to be, the only consideration shaping administrative and policy making decisions. We believe that client opinion can be systematically studied without necessarily assuming that the client is 'sovereign' or an 'economic man' who should be encouraged to 'shop around' in a market of social services. Perhaps, clients will desire forms of 'treatment' that the social work profession considers therapeutically unsound, detrimental to the client's social functioning, or unethical. In addition, matters unrelated to clients will inevitably enter into the decision-making process, e.g., the organizational demands of the agency offering the services, the demands of the profession as a whole, the expectations of relevant 'publics', especially those who provide moral and financial support. None the less, in the final analysis, client appraisals will, or at least should, be an important determinant of the kinds of services offered and their disposition.

It is thus striking to note that administrators and policy makers simply do not have access to information of this type, and for a very simple reason: it has not been collected. A survey of casework research—the bulk of which has been carried out in the United States—reveals that clients are rarely asked to appraise the effectiveness of the services received. When appraisals are made, it has consistently been the social worker, not the client, who has made the appropriate series of judgments[1] On some occasions, judgments of effectiveness have been made by the worker who has provided the service; in other instances, external social work judges, on the basis of the case record, have made the assessment; in still others, social work researchers have interviewed clients and, on the basis of the data collected, have judged whether improvement in social functioning occurred or not. Rarely, however, have the clients themselves been asked for their opinion.[2]

Of course, independent client studies could be seen as superfluous, on the simple assumption that the judgments of the practitioner and those of the client would coincide. This might seem a reasonable assumption, but, on inspection, it turns out to be in large measure wrong. A review of the few studies in which relevant comparisons can be made reveals marked disparities between the two sets of judgments.[3] Interestingly enough, research in psychotherapy, which is generally carried out by psychologists or psychiatrists and is far more extensive than casework research, reveals similar patterns.[4] Once again, we find a tendency for clients and practitioners to diverge in their judgments. In short, we can only agree with Dorothy Beck who, in surveying client-practitioner discrepancies, points to the 'critical importance of tapping client perception directly'.[5]

This absence of client-oriented studies, significantly enough, is beginning to be noted, at least in certain sectors. Thus, at a recent meeting of the National Association of Social Workers (U.S.), it was held that the profession has concentrated on how to deliver services 'with little regard for whether it is delivering anything of real significance to the people most in need of help'. The statement continues: 'Largely because of [this] social work now faces a major crisis: the crisis of its relevance to the human condition.'[6]

Turning to England, it is germane that both the Younghusband and Seebohm reports have been taken to task on occasion for their failure to conduct consumer research. For example, Sinfield, in a recent overview of social work and its role in society, finds 'Seebohm's disregard for the potential or past customer of the social services . . . disturbing'. He goes on to add: 'Perhaps it is even more remarkable, or ironic, or just revealing, that the committee set up to assess the most appropriate training for community work, and chaired by Dame Eileen Younghusband, not only undertook no consumer research (perhaps because it was thought to be too expensive) but also made no reference to the lack of such enquiries—as if indeed they were of no relevance.'[7] An earlier statement by Barbara Wootton echoes very much the same sentiments:

> One cannot but wonder sometimes what 'clients' think of 'caseworkers'. Into this field, however, research workers on both sides of the Atlantic seem to be reluctant to penetrate. The Younghusband Committee made a pious but empty gesture in this direction. They 'would have liked to have undertaken a complementary inquiry into the reactions of those using the services'; but time (perhaps fortunately) did not allow. In the Rodgers-Dixon survey, a chapter is devoted to *Attitudes to Social Work*.[8] In this we learn about the attitudes of the social workers themselves to their work and to one another and about the views of the heads of the departments in which they are employed: but about

the reactions of those who experience their services not a word is said—save for one hint in an incidental reference to the work of Young and Willmott in East London. . . .[9]

Statements such as these leave little doubt that the absence of client studies is being felt, at least in some circles. It seems painfully clear, too, that once they are undertaken administrators, planners, and others will be in a better position to deploy social work resources more effectively.

The improvement of services

In comparison with administrators and policy makers, researchers are more oriented to improving the quality of future services.* There is increasing recognition that this involves finding answers to the following question: What kinds of activity on the part of therapists produce what kinds of change in what kinds of patients?[10] We say 'increasingly' because the thinking and approaches of researchers have recently been undergoing a re-orientation. Formerly, researchers were inclined to look upon therapeutic intervention in a more undifferentiated manner. Thus, many efforts have been made to compare the effects of 'treatment' versus 'no treatment' or, in a global manner, the impact of different treatments with the hope of finding one which was the 'best'.[11] Today, we have come to realize that the question as originally formulated was too broad—in other words that the effectiveness of treatment in any given instance will depend on a variety of circumstances. As Kubie remarks, 'Could there possibly be any one process of treatment from which one would have any right to expect constant results when dealing with such different processes? We would not expect all "fevers" to yield to the same therapeutic manoeuvres, nor all headaches, nor all paralyses.'[12] Or, as Hyman and Berger put it, 'the question "Is psychotherapy effective?" leads to oversimplified confusion. It is analogous to asking, "Is higher education effective?" without specifying

* In this part of our discussion we shall be referring to researchers of psychotherapy as well as of casework. These two modes of helping, as Scott Briar notes, have a great deal in common. 'The Current Crisis in Social Casework', *Social Work Practice*, National Conference on Social Welfare, 1967 (New York: Columbia University Press, 1967).

what kind of higher education, practised by what kind of teachers on which students.'[13]

This re-orientation in approach appears to be the result of several factors. For one thing, undifferentiated studies of outcome consistently revealed that treatment had little effect, that is, over and above the effects 'spontaneously' occurring in the natural environment. Summarizing the findings of psychotherapy research, Frank writes: 'Statistical studies of psychotherapy consistently report that about two-thirds of neurotic patients and 40 per cent of schizophrenic patients improved immediately after treatment, regardless of the type of psychotherapy they have received, and the same improvement rate has been found for patients who have not received any treatment that was deliberately psychotherapeutic.'[14] Or, in the words of a social worker researcher, 'The results of evaluative studies of casework and other traditional forms of interpersonal helping have been consistently disappointing. Despite occasional methodological shortcomings, enough careful studies have been done to sustain the conclusion that, in general, it has not yet been demonstrated that casework and related forms of conventional helping are effective.'[15] To researchers and to practitioners convinced of their healing powers these results were discouraging, even demoralizing, and generated pressure for a reformulation of the issues involved. Recently matters have become crystallized in the realization that some people receiving psychotherapy improve greatly, others improve not at all, while still others become worse. Compared to those who have received no treatment—and this is the significant finding—there is a greater range of effects. Thus, Bergin in a pioneering paper, based on a re-examination of seven studies, points out, 'although there tends to be no difference in the average amount of change between experimentals and controls, there does tend to be a significant difference in *variability* of change. The criterion, or change, scores for treatment groups attains a much wider dispersion than do those of control groups, even though the mean change in both groups is quite similar. . . . These various data indicate that psychotherapy can make people considerably better off than control subjects. Therefore, contrary to the notions of some critics, psychotherapy can produce improvement beyond that which may occur due to spontaneous remission alone.'[16] Conclusions such as these indicate the need for investigating the conditions under which treatment is or is not effective and herald the end of undifferentiated studies of 'treatment effects'.

Another element undermining a global approach derives from the proliferation of new treatment approaches. It is no longer merely a question of psychoanalytic *vs.* client-centred *vs.* behavioural psychotherapy; or supportive *vs.* clarifying case-work; or individual *vs.* group therapy. A host of new treatment modalities has appeared in America,[17] due in large part to renewed efforts to reach the poor and the emergence of the community mental health movement. Thus, one readily finds references, for example, to role playing, psychodrama, socio-therapy ('personality adjustment through social action'); more recently 'amicatherapy'[18] and 'filial therapy'[19] have made their appearance. Over and above the spread in treatment modalities, 'therapy' is now being offered by a wider range of persons than ever before. Formerly, the therapeutic role fell primarily to the psychiatrist, psychologist or social worker. Today, however, they are being increasingly joined by nurses, teachers, volunteers, indigenous non-professionals, and so forth.[20] If it has had no other effect, this burgeoning of new practitioners has presumably terminated the search for the 'one' most effective way of helping troubled people.

The task of matching up different types of therapists, treatments, clients, and problems into therapeutically effective combinations is a long range objective and begins with a search for variables that are significantly related to outcome. Typically, the investigator wants to learn what specific elements in the situation are responsible for an improvement (or deterioration) in the client's functioning, however this may be defined. The search for significant variables, in turn, is comprised of two processes. First, the researcher must decide which elements in the situation are to be investigated. Next, he (or some other researcher) must assess the actual impact of the variable (or variables) selected.

However, when we look at the first part of this process, or more precisely, the *sources* from which variables later to be tested are drawn, a curious fact emerges. Rarely have the variables which are singled out for study been drawn from the client's experiential field. As far as we know there are few instances in which researchers have decided to study certain aspects of the casework situation as a result of talking with clients or having knowledge of their viewpoints. This no doubt derives in part from the fact that very few studies of the client's 'phenomenological world' have been undertaken. Thus, the researcher lacks a backlog of information which might prove useful in formulating his research. A semi-intensive search of the literature reveals very few studies dealing with, or even touching on, the client's world in the field of casework[21] and perhaps a dozen in that of psycho-therapy.[22]

The latter figure may seem large, but it is small indeed when one takes into account the energy researchers at present expend on other efforts. Thus, Strupp and Bergin, in their recent survey of psychotherapy research, were able to draw on approximately 2,500 references, a high proportion of which appeared since 1964.[23] Not only are explorations undertaken from the viewpoint of clients largely lacking, but one suspects that their absence is not felt, at least keenly. Thus, in the well-known three volume collection, *Research in Psychotherapy*, which has drawn together the writings and discussions of many prominent investigators, one finds not a single plea that studies of this type be undertaken.[24]

If the variables selected for attention are not drawn from the perspective of clients, from what sources *are* they drawn? Unfortunately, little is known about the influences, formal or informal, leading to the selection of independent variables. Matters of this nature are typically not reported in the research literature. Still, several suggestions can be made. For one thing, at any given moment in a field of scientific endeavour, certain ideas, variables, or conceptions are apt to be prominent. Perhaps they have entered the literature because they were the object of much research, or because they embody the thinking and assumptions of a given school of thought, or because they are currently espoused by an eminent investigator. In any event, this 'field of relevant considerations' tends to comprise the effective scope of the investigator and inevitably moulds his thinking when he comes to formulating research. Relevant, too, is the socio-political context. Research today is largely dependent on outside support, and this may lead the investi-gator to focus on immediate issues—ones which are 'fundable'—and to neglect those which might conceivably have greater 'pay-off' in the future. The agency, organization, or clinic in which the investigator works comprises another context that may influence the selection of variables. A social work agency, for example, may be interested in reaching more clients, possibly by reducing the duration of treatment or by adding non-professionals to its staff. Agency 'interests' of this type will quite likely mould the thinking of the researcher and lead him to focus on certain areas, problems and variables rather than others.

Client-oriented studies, in our view, would have several functions. For one thing, they might well sensitize researchers to 'new' considerations, or at least ones outside their current span of attention. Scattered findings from the few studies that have been undertaken lend weight to such expectations. To illustrate, several investigators found a tendency for clients who were successfully treated to assume the values or norms of their therapists. Thus, Leichter and Mitchell interviewed a group of second-generation Jews who were receiving casework treatment in New York and who, in keeping with their cultural background, were more emotionally involved with kin (especially parents and siblings) than were their workers.[25] At the conclusion of treatment—and this is the significant finding—a number of these clients believed (as did their workers) that 'it is healthy and normal for the nuclear family to function primarily as an independent unit'. Thus, one wife who used to voice all her complaints to her sisters said that 'she didn't have the understanding [prior to treatment] that these things *should* be discussed with her husband'.[26] A husband whose mother-in-law was part of the household became aware, as a result of treatment, that 'two people who are married *should* live alone'.[27] Another researcher also reports a tendency on the part of successfully treated patients to assimilate the values of their therapists. After noting that 'most therapists seem to take precautions to avoid influencing their patients' values in any way at all', he suggests, 'it may be that the therapist communicates his values to the patient in many unintended, subtle ways, even when trying to avoid doing so'.[28] These suggestions remind us that we can ill afford to cut ourselves off from the observations and insights the clients might provide. It is essential, in other words, that researchers keep the door open to 'new' variables, of which clients are an important source.[29]

Aside from bringing new considerations to light, client studies can help to refine what is currently known or believed to be true about treatment. In this connection, a growing number of research studies have pointed up the importance of certain factors. For example, Strupp and Bergin in their review of the literature, remark that 'the therapeutic climate produced by the therapist's personality (including prominently such variables as his empathy, warmth, respect, etc.) is indeed a potent therapeutic agent . . .'.[30] To illustrate further, there is strong evidence, both from casework[31] and psychotherapy research,[32] that clients are more apt to continue in treatment when they and their therapists share similar expectations. However, from a research point of view, it is not enough to know that factors such as these are important *in general*. One also wants to know about the *specific conditions under which* they are important and the processes leading to these results. Again, work previously undertaken can be used to illustrate the potential value of client studies. For example, Gleidman *et al.* found that patients who gave 'inappropriate' reasons for being in therapy (e.g., a desire to please or punish someone in their environment) were as likely to remain in treatment, and improve as much, as those giving 'appropriate' reasons (e.g., a desire to modify oneself). The authors conclude that 'where remaining in treatment favourably affects the equilibrium of a patient's present pattern of living, it is likely that he will remain in therapy'.[33] In our terms, the authors are suggesting that while congruency in expectations between worker and client may be 'important', under certain conditions its importance may be over-ridden by other considerations, as for example when clients have 'extramural' reasons for remaining in treatment. To illustrate further, group therapy is often held to be successful, among other reasons, because the participants learn, perhaps for the first time in their lives, that 'others have problems too'. In time, this becomes a source of comfort and perhaps insight as well. Yalom, however, found that in certain instances patients were *adversely* affected by hearing the problems of others. Some feared that they might become as mentally disturbed as others in the group. Another patient got upset because she felt that the other members were 'trying to heap their problems on top of hers'.[34] Once again, these findings (or clues) suggest ways in which client self-reports may refine broadly based generalizations—in this instance, ones concerning the helpfulness of learning about other people's problems.

Finally, the case for client studies can be put in terms of the alternatives available to a researcher who is both free from the kinds of constraints noted and who is intent on locating variables significantly related to outcome. Theoretically, he could proceed by trial and error. That is, he might focus on and then submit to empirical test any variables that came to his attention, whether they were connected with the practitioner, the client, the interaction between them, the nature of treatment, or whatever. Such a procedure, however, has little to recommend it. Potentially, the number of variables that might be relevant is unlimited, which means that the investigator—given his random, grossly inductive approach—has little chance of locating significant factors. It is always possible, of course, that he will turn out to be lucky—he might stumble on something important. The odds, however, are against him. In fact, to proceed in this manner is to forfeit one of the few advantages that the behavioural sciences have over the physical. Physical particles, chemical substances, and other inanimate things cannot reveal why they respond as they do to certain stimuli or influences. Human beings can, and not to capitalize on this is the height of complacency, if not recklessness.

We do not assume, of course, that clients will always be able to supply the researcher with useful or enlightening information. In some instances, clients may be partially unaware of their 'real' feelings or their reasons for feeling as they do. Moreover, even if aware, they may be reluctant to reveal them. Finally, certain clients are unlikely to be good informants under any conditions, for example, severely disturbed adults. Despite limitations of this type, the self-reports of clients should prove valuable. Whatever else might be said, clients are apt to know a good deal more about their thoughts, beliefs, experiences, and reactions to treatment than do those who are trying to help them. The authors of a recent American study have summed the matter up well: 'Actually there is a great deal of logic in using [clients] directly rather than workers or research interviewers as the chief judges of outcomes. They are the consumers of the service. It is they who define their problems and choose where to go for help. It is they who directly experience the helping process and live daily with the results of that help. Only they can really say whether as a result they are or are not better able to cope with their particular problems.... Clients can also report what went wrong, if anything, and why they terminated. They can likewise report what more they needed and did not receive.'[35] In a similar connection, we are reminded of the Newsons' recent research in Nottingham, concerned with four-year-olds and their mothers. Instead of relying on 'tortuous' psychological tests—allegedly a common practice in psychology, according to the authors—they questioned the mothers *directly* about their feelings and attitudes. In commenting on this 'departure', they remark, 'Often the status of the individual as a thinking person, with the possibility both of making his own insights and of voluntarily supplying material which will allow others to make insights, seems to be mislaid on the way.'[36] This, as we have tried to suggest, is no less true of social work clients than of mothers.

Sources of neglect

The failure of social work researchers to undertake client-oriented studies comprises a fascinating chapter in the sociology of research. How does it happen, in other words, that we do not have countless studies of clients—investigations which depict in detail their preconceptions of treatment, their actual experiences, their reactions to what occurred, their assessments of whether it was helpful, their views as to why it was helpful or not and so forth? The question is to the point for several reasons. First, in terms of research strategies, the generic importance of exploring the actor's perceptions and viewpoints is well recognized. Barton and Lazarsfeld state the rationale for such studies:

In exploring for possible factors affecting some given variable [such as the outcome of treatment], or for chains of causes and effects constituting a 'process', there appear to be two basic techniques. The first attempts to obtain objective information about the sequence of events, particularly what events preceded the response under investigation. . . .

The second technique is to ask people themselves to explain what happened and to give their reasons for acting as they did. The basic question here is always 'why?' This technique has obvious limitations: people are often unaware of the real motives, of indirect influences, of the precise chain of causes and effects, of underlying necessary conditions. On the other hand it stands to reason that the participant knows a good deal about his own behaviour, particularly about attitudes, motives, influences, 'trigger events', and so on, and often can tell the outside investigator about things which he would never have guessed by himself. 'Reasons' may not be the whole story, but they are an important source of information on possible factors and in some cases a quite indispensable source, especially in the early stages of investigation.[37]

Not only are there compelling theoretical reasons for under-taking such research, but a great many studies have, in fact, been undertaken. Within sociology, investigations of this type have had a long tradition. The researches of Thomas and Znaniecki,[38] Shaw,[39] and other members of the 'Chicago School', dating back forty or fifty years or so, systematically took into account the actor's perspective, viewing this as an important means of shedding light on the situation at hand as well as identifying significant variables for future study. Since then a fairly regular procession of such studies has appeared. One might mention Robert Merton's *Mass Persuasion* (1946)[40] which, in investigating why a radio 'marathon' conducted by Kate Smith was so successful in selling war bonds, relied heavily on open-ended interviews with listeners of the programme; or Donald Cressey's *Other People's Money* (1953)[41] in which auto-biographical accounts of embezzlement are provided by the embezzlers themselves; or Fred Davis' *Passage Through Crisis* (1963)[42] in which polio victims and their families relive their hospital experiences; or a more recent study by James Carey (1968)[43] which is concerned with drug usage as reported by drug users. Leaving sociology aside, market research comprises another area which has made extensive use of 'client-oriented' studies. For example, it is common knowledge that many business enterprises systematically canvass the opinions of potential buyers. Lack of research precedent, in other words, cannot account for why social work researchers have not solicited the opinions of clients. How then can the absence of such research be explained? There are probably many reasons but four will be considered at this point.

First, social work thinking is heavily infused with psycho-analytic concepts and viewpoints and has been ever since the 1920's, most notably in the United States. Whatever the merits of this approach, it has encouraged practitioners to discount or explain away views the client might express. As the editor of a recent psychoanalytic symposium remarked:

> Psychiatry has always undervalued the capacities of the patient, has tended to regard his views as at worst, meaningless, or at best, the unbalanced and exaggerated preoccupations of an over-sensitive soul—in any event, the views of an unreliable witness. And the patient undergoing psychoanalysis has not escaped this judgement. In part, no doubt, the fact that the psychoanalyst is preoccupied with the patient's distorted, as opposed to valid, perceptions leads him to take such a view, but one suspects that a question of status is involved: that the therapist is unconsciously betrayed into an assumption of superiority of judgement, and the patient's capacity for accurate perception is correspondingly marked down. If this prejudice were to be overcome the evidence gained from patients about their families might be taken more seriously.[44]

The modern social worker is by training inveterately suspicious of appearances, and so she judges that the client cannot perceive clearly and without distortion the reality of the treatment situation. The client's appraisal of the services offered (especially if negative) and his reasons for feeling as he does are apt to be viewed as epi-phenomena, as derivations of his underlying problem and the manner in which he has related to the worker. Cognitive elements, in brief, are looked upon as having little independent validity of their own. While psychoanalytic thinking is being increasingly challenged today by other orientations, it is still pervasive and presumably leads social work researchers (most of whom in America have received social work training) to question the value of client studies.[45]

Second, the social worker's desire for professional status very likely constitutes another influence contributing to the absence

THE NEGLECTED CLIENT 15

of client studies. One of the hallmarks of a profession is that the practitioner, because of skills derived from a body of abstract knowledge, can discern what is best for the client. It is in fact on this basis that Greenwood differentiates customers from clients. Extending his observations slightly, we can say that a customer believes he knows his own needs, will shop around in an effort to satisfy them, and feels confident in judging the value of the merchandise offered. By and large the seller accepts this definition, which is epitomized by the slogan: 'The customer is always right!' On the other hand, the professional, according to Greenwood, 'dictates what is good or evil for the client, who has no choice but to accede to professional judgment. Here the premise is that, because he lacks the requisite theoretical background, the client cannot diagnose his own needs or discriminate among the range of possibilities for meeting them. Nor is the client considered able to evaluate the calibre of professional service he receives.'[46]

An investigation of clients' perceptions may be threatening to the professional to the extent that it is construed as a challenge to his competence. This may be particularly so in the case of social workers in view of the precarious state of social work knowledge and their determined efforts to become professionalized.[47] As a result, efforts to explore social work practice, and most especially if this involves talking to clients, may be, and is in fact, strongly resisted on some occasions, a matter to which we shall return. In passing, it is interesting to note that sociologists who, for the purposes of a survey, need measures of their respondents' mental health are apt to rely on self-ratings[48]—a practice which has been eschewed by clinicians (or researchers who were formerly clinicians). No doubt this difference in methodology derives in part from the demands of survey research; it is frequently necessary to interview many persons and directly asking individuals to evaluate their mental health (or happiness) is an economical way of securing an assessment. But it may also reflect the fact that sociologists, unlike mental health practitioners (or ex-practitioners), are in no sense responsible for the psychological functioning of the population surveyed. In a sense, their lack of accountability may free them to use measuring devices which would be threatening to others.

Thirdly, the structure of social work services would seem to comprise another relevant consideration. Social work clients (omitting those in residential treatment centres, group therapy, etc.) are typically isolated from each other. Characteristically they come to an agency, usually in an urban setting, possibly catch a glimpse of each other but never meet again. By contrast, 'clients' who find themselves in other organizations such as mental hospitals, prisons and schools *do* interact.[49] Should they become dissatisfied with the services offered, they are apt to become rapidly apprised of each other's attitudes and in turn unite and demand changes. At this point, their 'custodians', if placed under sufficient pressure, may grant concessions. But, concurrently they may also make earnest efforts to understand the outlook of the dissenters. It is presumably no accident that prison riots, student rebellions and the like often result in inquiries tapping the perspectives of those 'in revolt'.

The situation is strikingly different in social work: client grievances are apt to remain privatized and unexpressed. Admittedly changes are under way, particularly in the area of housing and public assistance. Both in England[50] and the United States[51] clients are becoming organized and are demanding, sometimes through 'sit-ins', marches, or demonstrations, changes of one kind or another. But, in comparison with 'clients' who interact on a regular rather than emergency basis, the structural isolation of *social work* clients is rather complete. This very fact, in our opinion, undercuts an important source of motivation for client studies.

Finally, let us turn to a very different type of consideration. It is our impression that exploratory studies have relatively low status in social work research circles.[52] In a mistaken view of the manner in which scientific knowledge accumulates, social work researchers have tended to identify research exclusively with the techniques required to carry it out, especially those needed for rigorous quantitative studies.[53] Thus, the research literature is replete with discussions of experimental design, measurement, criteria of outcome, the reliability of judgments, the use of statistics, and so forth. Perhaps this over-emphasis on 'hardware' derives from the fact that social work researchers are anxious to appear 'scientific' and to differentiate themselves from the 'softness' of the casework material collected by their colleague practitioners. In any event, the pre-occupation with technical matters, or as Greenwood has put it, 'the tendency to regard operational research as comprising the whole of social work research'[54] has seemingly drawn attention away from the study of clients, at least in so far as exploratory, loosely formulated studies are called for at this point. The invidious distinctions attached to different research procedures have, it would appear, left clients unstudied.

2

The nature of the study

Research workers wishing to interview social work clients are immediately confronted with a considerable obstacle: how to gain access to them. In the past, social agencies, in Britain and the United States, have been extremely reluctant to grant researchers direct access to clients, particularly if the researchers are not employees of the agency and are not members, professionally speaking, of the social work community. Such reluctance will require extensive reappraisal in the light of the twin emphases placed by the Seebohm Report on research and on the significance of consumer reaction in the social services.

Agency reluctance has typically taken one of three forms, justifiably or not. First, it is often held that simply facilitating contact between researchers and clients constitutes a breach of confidentiality on the part of the caseworker, and would thus be unethical. Secondly, research interviewing, it is held, may in some way damage the worker's relationship with the client. It seems to be assumed both that the relationship between social worker and client is a tender, easily bruised growth and that the research worker's interviewing will inevitably be clumsy. In his recent review of social work research, Massarik writes: 'There is considerable feeling in the social work community, perhaps particularly by casework practitioners, that to "do research" on the client *while he is a client* may be a dangerous practice; the assumption is that to use the client as a "guinea pig" while he is involved in a helping relationship with the agency interferes with the helping process itself.'[1] In this connection, social workers have objected to clients taking standardized psychological tests on the grounds that this might impede the establishment of a casework relationship.[2] Thirdly, it is sometimes held that research interviewing would prove emotionally upsetting for the client. If the interviewing takes place while the client is still in treatment, the worker's therapeutic task would allegedly become more difficult: he would not only have to cope with the client's original difficulty but also with the additional disturbances created by the researcher. If the research interviewing takes place after the case has closed, it might (allegedly) still prove unsettling for the client, in the sense of re-opening old wounds. It might force him to recall old grievances and to re-experience the anguish he suffered in trying to deal with them.

In view of the possibility of all or any one of these obstacles arising, we were fortunate indeed that the Family Welfare Association was interested in the kind of research we wished to undertake and was willing to grant access, with suitable safeguards, to people who had recently been clients. The Family Welfare Association (FWA) is a very old agency, the direct successor to the Charity Organisation Society founded in 1869. At the time of our research, the FWA was organized into six area offices, located in different parts of London, with an additional headquarters staff consisting of the main administration and a casework consultant. The agency employs about thirty-five social workers all of whom are professionally qualified[3] and who carry on the average thirty to thirty-five cases at any one time. Roughly speaking, the total caseload of the agency at any given time falls between 1,000 and 1,200 cases. It might also be added that the FWA is an important training agency with 60 per cent of the staff involved in the training of students.

The Family Welfare Association, then, is an active, well staffed organization. From the point of view of our research it had further advantages. First, for some years now the agency has systematically collected information with respect to its clients, and this data proved helpful from a research point of view. Secondly, the clients who come to the FWA come of their own volition and are thus 'free' to accept or reject the help that is offered. Since clients do not as a rule come because of pressure exerted by statutory agencies, their reactions to the casework situation are not complicated by questions of statutory enforcement. Thirdly, the Family Welfare Association is a family service. At a time when there is a trend in both America and Britain towards accepting the family as the focus of social work help, it seemed appropriate to begin our exploration at a point where it would be most likely to make some contribution to future developments. As far as Britain is concerned, the clients we interviewed from the Family Welfare Association are likely to be the kind who will in the future be coming to the newly established local authority family services.

Obtaining the subjects

Our main aim was to interview a group of clients to learn something of their perceptions of, and reactions to, the casework services received. We were especially interested in the conditions that had led them to feel either satisfied or dissatisfied with the help received. With this end in view, we hoped to obtain two distinct groups of clients—the satisfied and the dissatisfied. Actually the more extreme they turned out to be in their reactions, the better it would be for our purposes, in that the factors responsible for their feelings would presumably stand out more clearly and thus be more visible to an outside observer. In brief, the study was very definitely conceived as exploratory. We hoped to elicit from the interviewees a relatively complete account of their experiences at the FWA, as seen from their perspective. The degree to which their experiences are typical of FWA clients, or more broadly casework clients in the U.S. or England, is an entirely separate question that cannot be answered on the basis of exploratory studies such as this.

In an effort to obtain satisfied and dissatisfied clients— approximately an equal number of each—we decided to select cases in terms of how they were classified at closure, of which there are three possibilities: 'closed by joint agreement', 'terminated by worker', and 'client failed to continue'. We felt that if we interviewed clients whose cases had closed on their initiative ('failed to continue'), we would very likely encounter dissatisfied clients. Conversely, interviews with subjects whose cases had closed on the basis of a 'joint agreement' between worker and client would purportedly put us in touch with satisfied clients. This eliminated from consideration cases which had closed 'at the initiative of the worker' (which, according to rough calculation, represented about 15 per cent of the agency caseload). We had little basis for suspecting how clients of this description might have felt about the services received; accordingly, rather than taking a chance on obtaining subjects who were lukewarm or indifferent about their experiences—neither markedly satisfied nor dissatisfied—we decided to eliminate them from consideration. We decided also to restrict our attention to clients who were born within the British Isles, since the reactions of 'non-natives' to social work are likely to be complicated by cultural differences, language problems and so forth. A study of the responses of those who are not native to Britain is of considerable importance, but is a subject that merits study in its own right. (Estimates suggest that clients of this description, as of the first half of 1967, constituted less than 10 per cent of the agency caseload.) Finally, we decided to restrict our attention to cases which had closed relatively recently, in other words to clients whose memory of their experiences had not had a chance to fade and become indistinct.

Our first efforts—and these lasted for some months—were directed to obtaining and interviewing dissatisfied clients. We began in June 1967 by listing all cases (exclusive of the foreign-born) that had closed at the initiative of the client from January to May that year. The only exception was that one interview cases were included *only* for the month of May, since those whose contact was more distant might have difficulty recalling their experience. The resulting list contained 122 names; it was then circulated to the various district offices for checking by the workers who had handled these particular cases. Subsequently, thirty-four names were removed for one of the following reasons: the client had died or had moved away without leaving a forwarding address; he had returned to the agency for further treatment, and it had been agreed that cases that re-opened would not be interviewed; the client's husband allegedly did not know his wife had sought help from the FWA, and in order to preserve her secret we felt it best not to approach her on behalf of the study.

Of the eighty-eight persons remaining on the list, interviews were sought with sixty-five. The difference in these two figures is partly due to matters of geography. Although the study interviewers were located in both North and South London, certain addresses were still rather inconvenient to reach, especially since two visits were often required, one to arrange the interview and another to conduct it. Accordingly, interviews with certain clients were not solicited. In addition, we tended to by-pass clients, if on the basis of data collected by the agency, they had sought help with a relatively circumscribed problem, e.g., housing. Problems of this type, it was felt, would be less revealing for our purposes than would those, for example, involving marital difficulties.

The sixty-five clients were then written a letter by the head of the Social Work Department. (If both husband and wife had been clients, an interview was sought with only the wife—unless the husband had been seen more frequently.) The letter, which is reproduced in Appendix I, described the study, asked for the clients' co-operation, gave assurances of confidentiality, and indicated that an interviewer would call unless they contacted the agency, specifying they did not wish to be interviewed. Each of the clients was offered a pound for his co-operation. Forty-six of the sixty-five individuals contacted were ultimately interviewed; three refused (two on the basis that they had 'nothing to say') while the remainder had either moved without leaving any forwarding address or turned out to be ineligible, i.e., born outside the British Isles.

The refusal rate, it is interesting to note, was very low (as was true also of the 'joint-agreement' clients). This, we suspect, was due largely to the following reasons. The onus of refusal was placed on the client, in the sense that the letter assumed he would participate unless he actively indicated otherwise; the interviewers had thought through, ahead of time, ways of dealing with hesitancies expressed at the doorstep; finally, the offer of a pound (which was never refused) was probably an important inducement as many clients were in dire financial straits.

The selection and interviewing of joint-agreement cases closely follows the procedures outlined and took place after the interviews with the 'dropouts' had been completed. Certain differences in procedure, however, should be noted. First, we decided to interview only fifteen joint agreement cases, as many of the dropouts were turning out to be satisfied, roughly half as it happened. Since we hoped to interview an approximately equal number of satisfied and dissatisfied clients, there was thus no need to seek out a great many additional clients of the former type. Secondly, we tried to obtain only clients whose cases had closed during the two most recent months, which at that time were June and July. Only respondents from North London were sought as our interviewer in South London was unable to continue with the project. Finally, only clients who had received at least three interviews were listed in the hope that this would put us in touch with clients who had been especially satisfied.

As before, there was a 'shrinkage' in the list of names compiled (which originally came to thirty), due primarily to clients having changed their residence or having returned to the FWA for more treatment. From the names that remained, fifteen clients were interviewed, there being only one refusal—a West Indian wife who in any case was ineligible to participate.

As it turned out, about a third of the joint-agreement cases proved to be dissatisfied and were thus analagous to the dropout cases who proved to be satisfied. While these so-called 'discrepant' cases are of considerable interest in themselves (and came as a surprise to us), they have no particular bearing on our research.[4] That is, we were not interested in dropout or joint-agreement cases *per se*, but only in so far as they might lead us to satisfied and dissatisfied clients—which they did, but in an unexpected way.

Characteristics of our subjects

The reader may wonder how the clients we interviewed compare to the agency caseload as a whole. Below are several comparisons between our subjects and the agency caseload, as measured by the total number of cases that closed from January to May 1967 inclusive. (Tabulations were made by us on the basis of data collected by the agency.)

1   *Areas from which clients came*

Our clients came disproportionately from areas 2 and 3 and were under-represented in area 5 and to a lesser extent in area 4. This is a direct outcome of differences in accessibility; as noted earlier, it was difficult for the interviewers to reach certain areas, as a result of which clients living in these areas were occasionally by-passed.

Percentage of FWA Clients Living in Different Areas of London

		Study Clients	All Clients (*Jan.–May 1967*)
		%	%
1	Hammersmith	13	12
2	Kensington, Chelsea	27	15
3	City, Islington, Tower Hamlets	25	15
4	Wandsworth	7	12
5	Lewisham	5	24
6	Lambeth, Southwark	23	22
		100% (N = 60)*	100% (N = 591)

* Information missing in one case

2 *Number of interviews received*

Our respondents tended to receive more interviews on the average, there being a marked under-representation of one interview cases in our group. This again is a direct result of certain decisions made earlier.

Percentage of FWA Clients Receiving Different Numbers of Interviews

Number of Interviews	Study Clients	All Clients (*Jan.–May 1967*)
	%	%
1	7	32
2	18	17
3–6	43	25
7–20	27	17
Over 20	5	9
	100% (N = 60)	100% (N = 591)

3   *Types of problems focused on*

The FWA collects information on the kinds of problems that workers have focused on during treatment. Considerable similarity between our cases and the total caseload is revealed by the figures below. For example, the two problems most frequently focused on in each instance involved 'marital discord' and 'economic difficulties'.

The main difference in the two distributions is the greater proportion of 'marital discord' cases in our group, 34 per cent *vs.* 19 per cent. (The table below should be read as follows: 'Of the 110 problems focused on by the workers who treated our clients, 34 per cent involved "marital discord".')

Problems Focused on by the Worker During Treatment

Type of Problems	Problems of Study Clients	Problems of All Clients (Jan.–May 1967)
	%	%
Marital Discord	34	19
Isolation	6	7
Physical Handicap or Illness	4	8
One Parent Family	7	7
Mental Disorder	3	5
Adolescence	2	2
Parent-Child Relationship	13	8
Economic Difficulties	23	25
Old Age	1	3
Housing	4	11
Other	4	4
	101% (N = 110)*	99% (N = 1081)*

* The number of problems exceeds the number of clients as more than one problem was sometimes focused on.

During the interviewing, we collected additional background data from our subjects. The material below will give the reader a clearer idea of our subjects.

1 Nine out of ten of the subjects were women (this imbalance partially deriving from our selection procedures). Nearly all of these individuals were, or had been, married (fifty-seven out of sixty-one).

2 This was clearly a predominantly working-class group[5]:

a Four out of five of the respondents left school at fifteen or younger and only one individual had gone to university.

b In three out of four cases, the head of the household was a manual worker. The fourteen respondents who fell in the non-manual categories tended to hold jobs requiring no great degree of skill or training, such as waiters, shop assistants, and telephone operators.

3 The median age of these individuals was thirty-four, with over half between twenty-five and forty.

4 Judged in terms of residential mobility, these individuals would probably be considered fairly stable. About a third of the subjects had been living in their present neighbourhoods for twenty years or more; a third from five to nineteen years; and a third for less than five years.

The interviewing process

A good deal of thought and experimentation went into the construction of the interview schedule. When we began the study we had certain general areas in mind which we wished to explore, but we did not know the best way to elicit relevant information. For example, which questions should be asked, in what order, how should they be phrased, when should we probe and so forth? The early interviews we conducted greatly clarified such matters, and in addition, they brought to light significant topics which we had overlooked and which were subsequently incorporated in the interview. For example, we came to see that it was important to explore the client's imagery of the worker's intent; that is, what, in the client's view, was the worker's objective in asking certain questions or in behaving in certain ways? Again, we came to recognize that clients seeking economic help sometimes felt like 'cadgers' and that this feeling played an important part in shaping their outlook and reactions to treatment. In brief, the interview schedule underwent revision, most particularly in the early stages when we were still feeling our way.

The interview schedule was divided roughly speaking into the following sections. After asking the client for certain factual information concerning his background (where he was brought up, his schooling, the composition of his present family, etc.), we asked him to describe the difficulties that had led him to the FWA and to indicate how he had earlier tried to cope with them. Next he was asked about any factors (over and above his distress) that led him to the FWA and the kind of help he expected to receive. The following section dealt with his experiences at the agency, and a variety of questions were framed around such topics as the following: his impressions of the worker; the kinds of topics he talked about at first and later on; the ways in which the worker responded; his imagery of what the worker was doing, etc. In the final section, the client was asked to assess his experiences at the agency and to pinpoint the ways in which he was helped or not helped, as the case might be.

In a study such as this, the quality of the interviewing plays a vital role in the study's success, and for this reason considerable effort went into the selection and training of the interviewers. In the early stages of the study, one of the authors (JM) spent considerable time with each of the interviewers, going over tape recorded interviews the latter had conducted. By and large the objective was to pinpoint weaknesses in the interviewer's approach and to develop ways of coping with troublesome situations that might arise. For example, in one interview the client, after being asked his impressions of the worker, said he 'had no impressions whatsoever' and we tried to work out ways of coping with such responses should they occur in the future.[6]

Speaking more generally there has been a failure, in our view, to recognize that qualitative interviewing is a highly demanding craft and requires a good deal more than establishing rapport. It is not enough, in other words, that the interviewer be a 'nice' person, 'interested' in what the respondent says and sensitive to his various moods and thoughts. Effective qualitative interviewing demands other qualities as well and here we would especially stress: an analytical aptitude, that is, an ability to dissect a respondent's answer in terms of its relevance for the question; resourcefulness in eliciting material from those who are inhibited, inarticulate, unclear in their thinking, given to irrelevancies, etc.; and a certain doggedness in persevering with the matter at hand. The need for such qualities becomes apparent when one takes into account the manner in which interviewees typically respond to open-ended questions. Even though respondents are able to formulate their thoughts and willing to convey them, they rarely provide an adequate answer—one that is both specific and complete—the first time a question is asked. They may misunderstand the question, or wander off at a tangent, or say they 'don't know', even though one suspects they do. Moreover, even if they *are* on the right track, their answers may be excessively vague. Or if precise, they may be restricted in scope. Those who undertake qualitative interviewing have to cope continuously with contingencies of this nature, and this is not an easy task.

One might parenthetically add that the interaction of every-day life is a very poor training ground for cultivating the skills required, in that individuals rarely question each other in a precise and exhaustive manner. Whether out of tact or disinterest, we typically settle for responses that are hazy, incomplete, or irrelevant. There is a kind of 'smoothing-out' process in everyday conversation which is the exact antithesis of the pointedness that is called for by qualitative interviewing.[7] In a sense, the effective qualitative interviewer must abandon the conversational conventions in which he has been reared.

Let us now turn to the conduct of the interview itself. The interviews were carried out in the home of the client, were tape recorded and lasted for about an hour and a half on the average. In about a half a dozen instances, the respondent was re-visited and was talked with, all told, for approximately three or four hours. Every effort was made to interview the respondent in private, that is, without other adults or older children (ones over four or five years) being present—in the belief that this would make for greater frankness. In some instances, however, we were unsuccessful: the respondent's spouse, who happened to be home at the time, wandered into the room and rather 'naturally' entered into the conversation. This rarely happened, however, and thus raises no particular questions from a research point of view.

In an exploratory study such as this, it is extremely important to obtain a complete account of the respondent's (and inter-viewer's) remarks. In this connection, our use of tape recorders was an indispensable aid and deserves some comment. The completed tapes provided us with a considerable amount of detail (each interview ran to about fifteen typed pages single-spaced, when transcribed); they enabled us to capture significant passing remarks which might otherwise have been lost; and they afforded us some insight into the client's feelings, in so far as these were revealed by his mode of expression, the affect connected with various remarks and so forth. In a written interview, the interviewer (assuming he cannot take shorthand) is forced to be selective and as a result a good deal of valuable material is bound to be lost. However, tape recorders have other assets as well, and these are worth noting. For one thing, they enable the interviewer to cover more ground during a comparable period of time. He need not slow down the pace of the interview in order to keep up with the respondent. Nor will the respondent, for his part, tactfully and spontaneously slow down in an effort to relieve the interviewer's plight. Secondly, the use of a tape recorder relieves the interviewer of the drudgery and distraction connected with writing and in so doing enables him to concentrate more fully on the matter at hand. Finally, we should add that tape recorders were readily accepted by all the persons we interviewed. As a matter of fact, several respondents, presumably accustomed to radio and TV documentary programmes, were disappointed to learn that their tapes would not be aired to a wider audience!

How much confidence can be placed in what the respondents told us? To begin with, it is germane to note that most of our subjects talked freely and at considerable length. We made it very plain both in the introductory letter and at the beginning of each interview that we had no official connection with the agency and that there was thus no possibility of the respondents being personally connected by the agency with anything they said. There was, accordingly, no reason why they should wish to hold back information or dissimulate. Aside from this, the topic of investigation was emotionally salient. Seeking help from an agency was an important event for most and they became highly involved in the questions we raised. Many, as a matter of fact, continued to talk about their experiences and reactions even after we had covered all the topics included in our schedule. Finally, the respondents frequently volunteered rather 'damaging' things about themselves, which also suggests that they were being as frank as they could and were not trying to cover up.

We should add that at certain points in the interview we intentionally returned to topics earlier dealt with, approaching them from a different angle, in order to ensure that we were obtaining reliable responses. For example, in addition to asking the subjects whether they felt they had been helped and if so in what ways, we also asked whether they would recommend the FWA to those with similar difficulties, and why they would or would not make such a recommendation. We were re-assured to find that their answers to multiple questions of this type were highly consistent which strongly suggests (though it admittedly does not prove) that we were obtaining 'truthful' responses.

There are, however, several possible sources of error or distortion of which the reader should be aware. Ours was a retrospective study which means that the respondents were asked to go back in time and recall their earlier feelings, percep-tions, and experiences. It is quite possible that the passage of time, bringing with it an involvement in fresh experiences, affected the accuracy of their recall. This may have particularly been so in the case of clients whose difficulties had undergone change since leaving the agency, but for reasons not connected with the agency. For example, in several instances, the clients' difficulties became aggravated (for reasons unconnected with the agency or treatment) and this may have led them to become more critical of their treatment experiences than would otherwise have been the case. Conversely, on several occasions, the clients' difficulties improved and this may have led them to recall their treatment experiences with a mellowness they did not feel at the time. In order to guard against recall errors of this type, we intentionally selected clients whose contact with the agency had been relatively recent. None the less, the possi-bility of distortion, at least in certain cases, remains.

Finally, at various points in our study we attempt to depict what the workers were actually doing and saying, and here we have largely relied on the accounts supplied by the clients. There are clearly a number of hazards in this procedure. For one thing, our subjects were not trained observers. More im-portant, they were undergoing a good deal of emotional stress during treatment—both because of their problems and the situation they were in—and this may have affected their objectivity. Quite possibly certain things the workers did or said became unduly magnified in their eyes, others forgotten, still others distorted. There are, however, grounds for placing a certain amount of credence in the accounts which the clients supplied. We were encouraged to find a good deal of similarity in their reports. That is, various clients were independently telling us the same things about their respective workers. In addition, we obtained some confirmation from the workers themselves. As we shall point out in the following section, nine of the workers who had handled various of the clients talked with had been interviewed themselves and their description of their procedures closely parallels that supplied by the clients.

Interviews with the workers

After we had completed our client interviews, we talked with nine of the social workers who had interviewed clients in whom we were especially interested (they represented just under a third of the total of thirty workers involved in our cases). We hoped to elicit two types of information from them—their perceptions of the treatment situation and of the client's perceptions. The interviews—carried out by one of the authors (NT) and tape recorded—were loosely structured, and as a rule did not follow any set format, since they had to be adapted to the client whose particular case was under review. In general, however, the following questions were explored: How did the worker visualize (diagnose) the client's problems? What were his treatment objectives and how did he try to achieve these? How did he account for the fact that the client dropped out (when this was the case)? What, in his opinion, did the client expect from treatment? Was the client satisfied or dissatisfied with the services received? Did he feel he had been helped, and if so in what ways? (While the workers knew we had interviewed these particular clients, they were not told anything about the latters' responses.)

It would have been valuable if we had been able to invest more time in this phase of the study, which would have included carrying out a greater number of interviews with the workers involved. Unfortunately, however, this was precluded by lack of resources and time, and the fact that a number of workers who had treated clients in our group had earlier left the agency. Nonetheless, the interviews which we did carry out proved to be very useful (despite the fact that we only explicitly refer to them at several points in the text). As already noted, they enabled us to check on the clients' version as to what was 'objectively' happening during treatment—that is, the kind of things the worker was doing and saying. They also enabled us to obtain a fuller understanding of the ways in which misunderstandings develop and spiral in the casework situation. In this sense, they were similar to having information about both, rather than merely one, of two partners involved in a marital conflict. Finally, there are a number of points at which these interviews reassured us that we were on the right track in reaching certain conclusions or drawing certain inferences about our clients.

Plan of the study

The study is divided into two parts, the first concerned with the factors leading the clients to the FWA. As will become apparent, the persons we interviewed felt 'desperate' before coming to the agency, and their distress was unquestionably a key factor in leading them to seek help. Nonetheless, other influences were also present, and it is these that occupy our attention. Specifically, Chapter 3 focuses on the client's friends and relatives and delineates ways in which (intentionally or otherwise) they moved the respondent closer to the agency. Chapter 4 centres on various persons who drew the FWA to the client's attention; we are interested here in the role which these 'referral agents' played in initiating treatment.

The following and major part of the study focuses on the conditions responsible for the client's satisfaction or dissatisfaction with the services received. However, before outlining the specific chapters involved, it is essential to call attention to several categorizations that are integral to our analysis.

First, it can come as no surprise that respondents were classified in terms of whether they were satisfied or dissatisfied. This turned out to be a very simple task. By and large, these clients had strong feelings about their experiences at the FWA, and they were not the least bit hesitant in revealing them. As a matter of fact, the interviewer generally knew precisely how the client felt long before formal questions concerning his reactions were broached. The topic was very salient for them. It was as though they could hardly wait to tell us exactly how they had felt.

This, however, was not invariably the case. There were some whose reactions were milder and who had to deliberate before answering questions concerning their reactions. Rather than being slightly positive or slightly negative about *everything* that had happened, the client's reactions in these instances tended to be a blend of pros and cons. For example, several clients were appreciative of the agency's efforts to help them, but dismayed by the lack of results. In other instances, help was provided by the FWA (generally material assistance) but the client was disturbed by the processes preceding its dispensation. By and large, however, our cases are relatively 'pure' in the sense that cross-currents of this type are fairly rare. We are thus in the fortunate position of having a group of respondents who felt strongly about their experiences.

There is one other dichotomy that plays an important role in our analysis, although its importance was far from apparent at first. By and large, clients came to the agency with one of two purposes in mind. They either wanted help in dealing with someone else, generally a spouse, sometimes a child, and, on one occasion, a neighbour. Or they wanted 'material assistance' of some kind which we have defined broadly to include: clients who sought money or goods (either outright or in the form of a loan); those who wanted help in dealing with creditors or landlords; those who sought aid in getting better housing, etc.

There were several occasions in which clients sought both types of help and when this was the case the client was classified in terms of what appeared to be his primary purpose in coming to the agency. We should also add that there were four clients who do not fit into either of the two categories utilized. These were either clients who were hoping to establish contact between the agency and a troubled person in their environment (to whose difficulties they could have in no way contributed) and those who were seeking specialized information and nothing more, e.g., a woman who wanted information regarding the mechanics of obtaining a divorce.

The importance, from our standpoint, of the two help-seeking categories mentioned derives from the fact that each is integrally related to certain of the clients' earlier thoughts and feelings. To be more precise, one cannot adequately understand the reactions of these clients to treatment unless one has a firm grasp of the various beliefs, feelings and expectations which they brought into the treatment situation and which were firmly rooted in their thinking before they crossed the threshold of the FWA. Significantly, however, the preconceptions of those who sought material assistance differed in important ways from those who sought interpersonal help. Those who sought material assistance felt humiliated at having to go to the agency and expected that their experiences would be anything but pleasant. Those who sought help in dealing with someone else, while not humiliated at the prospect of seeking help, anticipated that their difficulties would be handled in a certain manner. In each instance, the client's reactions were significantly affected by the degree to which the worker's behaviour conformed to his particular expectations.

The chapter divisions in the second part of the book grow out of these considerations. Chapters 5 and 6 focus on clients who sought help in dealing with someone else, while Chapters 7, 8 and 9 are concerned with those who sought material assistance. Each of these two groupings is further subdivided in terms of whether clients' experiences were a source of satisfaction or dissatisfaction.

One final word concerning our handling of interview excerpts. As anyone who has worked with verbatim material knows, written transcripts are studded with distractions of one kind or another, e.g., superfluous phrases, false starts, twisted constructions, etc. In the interests of readability and coherence distractions of this type have been deleted or changed whenever this could be done without altering the substance of what was said. Moreover, in lengthy, free-flowing interviews of the type we conducted, it frequently happens that interviewees will return to topics previously touched on, providing further illustrations, extending their thoughts, or maybe qualifying them in some way. In a number of instances we consolidated these passages, in the interests of providing a more complete and faithful picture of the client's thoughts and feelings.

Towards the meeting of client and agency

3

The inadequacy of informal resources

Among the important assumptions made at the beginning of the study was the following: to a significant degree, people will try to cope with their personal problems by seeking help from their interpersonal environment, particularly friends and relatives. We went on to reason that if an individual did not receive help which, in his view, was suitable, he would more likely seek help from another source. In other words, we felt that an individual's decision to seek professional help would be a function, in part, of his earlier interactions with his confidants or 'lay' helpers.[1]

This view of help-seeking departs somewhat from earlier formulations. Mental health practitioners and researchers, in the past, have tended to look upon help-seeking as though it were a choice of either seeking professional assistance or going without help of *any kind*. Such a view entirely overlooks the role played by friends and relatives in the problem-coping process. American experience suggests that informal, non-professional helpers are more widely consulted than all the specialists combined (e.g., doctors, clergymen, mental health workers).[2] According to one survey, Americans were thirteen times more likely to take worries which 'they didn't know what to do about' to informal, rather than formal, problem-solving agents.[3] Moreover, there is undoubtedly an overlap in the therapeutic functions performed by the two sets of problem-solvers; friends as well as social workers, for example, are apt to offer emotional support to those who are distraught. In our view, it is useful to place informal *and* professional methods of problem coping under the same conceptual umbrella and to look upon them as alternative ways of dealing with difficulties. Once this is done, it can reasonably be argued that an inadequacy in one area (explicitly, the informal) will induce tendencies to utilize the other (the formal or professional).

These notions in no way lessen the importance of other determinants of seeking professional help. Evidence suggests, for instance, that troubled persons are more apt to seek professional help if they are in great distress; if they understand and endorse the therapeutic beliefs of mental health specialists; if professional resources are available in their vicinity; if they are aware of these resources and so forth.[4] Still, what these persons ultimately do will also depend on their appraisals of, and reactions to, the particular problem-solving resources currently available to them in their informal milieu.

In order to explore these matters, our respondents were asked a series of questions about their informal network—its composition; in whom, if anyone, they confided; why they did or did not confide in other people; the effects of their disclosures and so forth. Our aim was not to measure precisely the importance of gaps in the network in fostering contact with the FWA. We were more concerned at this stage with exploring the various ways in which a network might be deficient.

The material collected was eventually grouped in terms of what might be called communication 'deficiences' between the respondent and possible confidants. Roughly speaking, three types of 'deficiences' came to light: the respondent had no confidants; he had possible confidants but chose not to confide in them, at least fully; he confided in them but found their responses inadequate for some reason. In this chapter we shall examine these patterns, occasionally going into some detail in view of the dearth of material available on the topic and its likely importance for patterns of professional help-seeking.

All of the respondents were asked if they had any relatives or friends to whom they felt close and if so, how many. Nine out of ten could name at least one such person. On the average, however, the number of persons to whom they felt close was relatively small—generally two or three, usually relatives.[5]

Plainly, few of our respondents were completely isolated from potential confidants, only one out of ten. Those who were in this position typically comprised wives who had grown up some distance from London (often Ireland); after marriage, they had lost touch with their families and had made no new friends. Several other respondents, we should add, *were* close to their families, but did not anticipate a sympathetic response to any attempt to confide in them. One wife described her mother as a 'pull yourself together merchant', meaning that her mother could not tolerate 'helplessness' or 'weaknesses' of any type. Another wife told us that her family had disapproved of her marriage and that if she were to turn to them now for comfort or advice, they would say, 'Well, what did you expect? That's just like him!' While these persons, technically speaking, were 'close' to others, in terms of disclosure possibilities they were as isolated as those first mentioned.

Factors curbing communication

Let us now turn to the large majority—clients who were close to other persons who, in all likelihood, would respond sympathetically to their plight. There were a number of reasons why these persons were not confided in, at least fully, even though they might appear ideal 'on paper'.

Normative Restraints First, social norms applicable over a wide spectrum of society enjoin individuals to be self-reliant rather than dependent on others. These norms, which, of course, govern many aspects of our lives, and not just the matter at hand, restrained certain clients from revealing their difficulties. Comments such as the following are typical: 'I believe that what goes on in my house is my and my husband's business.' One of the few middle class clients interviewed referred to the 'stiff upper lip tradition' in which she had been raised.

In some instances, the respondent's inhibitions were increased by the specific nature of his difficulties. Personal difficulties vary in terms of their discussibility, and differences in discussibility, one suspects, are ultimately traceable to social norms. In any event, respondents were sometimes embarrassed to talk about their particular problems with others, close though they might be; for example, a wife who worried that her husband might be a homosexual, another who suspected

4—TCS

that her husband might be mentally ill. The sensitivity connected with such issues comprised an additional source of normative restraint.

Loss of Face Some respondents worried that their reputations or social appearance would suffer if others knew about their troubles. Mrs Stanton, for example, felt that if others knew of her husband's interest in another woman they would conclude that she had failed as a wife. 'I didn't want to discuss these things with my parents or sister. It's something that you want to keep to yourself. Let's be honest—it's not the type of thing you like everyone to know. It's hurt pride, because you've failed somewhere.' Mrs Farrell, although she confided in friends, did not reveal all, for fear of being labelled a 'pitiful' object:

> I told my friends what Brian had done to me, but I never bared my soul to them. I told them that I was upset and angry, but I didn't really let them know how much I minded, how it really hurt. . . . Why didn't I tell them? I suppose it boils down to the fact that they would look down on me and think what a stupid fool! Fancy putting up with that! I know that's the way *I* felt when I found out about my friend Dorothy and the way her husband had been treating her. I didn't exactly look down on her—I felt sorry for her when I found out what she'd put up with. But at the same time, I thought you silly fool! I thought that if he'd been my husband, he'd have my toe up his backside! Instead of taking it all and crying about it, I'd have put up a fight . . . I didn't mind my friends feeling sorry for me up to a point, but I didn't want them to pity me. I didn't want them to say, 'Anybody can walk over her'.

Mrs Lawton's reasons for maintaining silence were somewhat different. She believed that if others realized how her husband treated her, they would conclude there was something wrong with her. 'I was too ashamed actually to talk about my problems to friends and relatives. I just thought that if somebody [i.e., her husband] could treat me that way, there must be something wrong with me, something inferior.' In passing, it is interesting to note that not all wives were like Mrs Lawton; that is, not all felt their husbands' maltreatment of them would lead them to become stigmatized in the eyes of others and for this reason they were not reticent about revealing their difficulties. Mrs Carter, for example, told us that her husband treated other persons poorly too, and that this was common knowledge, particularly to members of his family.

> I always told Lily—my husband's sister—exactly what was going on. She said she knows that it is not my fault, she knows it's nothing to do with me, and she thinks he'll always be like that. Because before he was married he was always drinking and always had a tendency to hit people if they got him down. Because he used to hit his sisters. And his mother—he used to throw his dinner at her when he didn't want it.

The subject's willingness to reveal her troubles apparently stemmed from a belief that others (in this case her sister-in-law) would not come to think less of her as a result.

Projected Inability to Help Difficulties were sometimes withheld from friends and relatives because their expected responses would be of little help. For one thing, the prospective confidant might not have lived through a situation similar to the one confronting the client. Mrs Crew was very troubled about her relationship with her husband, but while she discussed this with her friends, she privately felt the kind of help they could give was severely limited. 'One of my friends is very happily married, so she is in no position to give any advice to someone who was going through my kind of problem. My other friend is a maiden lady and would not give me any advice for that reason. I talked to them; I had known them for a long while, but they could not advise me about my problem.' Similarly, Mrs Wilcox who had been deserted by her husband, remarked, 'It's no good talking about that side of it to anybody who has not experienced it, because they do not know anything about it. Now take my mother. She had been widowed, but that's a different experience entirely. . . .' It was assumed by respondents such as these that only those who have lived through a comparable, if not identical, experience can be helpful. Significantly, this notion sometimes led clients to question sharply the social worker's ability to help them, a point to which we shall return later.

The view was sometimes expressed that if confidants are to

be helpful, they must be impartial, particularly in difficulties involving more than one person. However else relatives might be viewed, they were *not* considered impartial and for this reason left much to be desired as confidants. Mrs Lawton felt that friends and relatives might just 'be sticking up for her against her husband', and not giving her the 'right judgment'. Several wives who were very close to their husbands' families considered discussing their difficulties with them. On second thought, however, they backed away, suspecting that an inherent bias would ultimately lead these relatives to side with their husbands. Sometimes, the respondent was close to both sets of parents but turned to neither for help:

> I thought to myself, well how can I go to my mother-in-law and tell her and ask for her help when I'm leaving her son. And then I thought to myself, if I go to my own mother, she'll just put the blame on to my husband and that'll make it more difficult. Because I'm her daughter, it's natural. You're their own and you can't do the wrong. So that just makes matters worse. So I thought it was better to talk to a stranger—because he's got nothing to do with you and he can tell you whether you're right or wrong or whether your husband is. (Mrs Stone)

On occasion, the respondent was seeking a specific type of help which, it was felt, members of the network could not provide. Chief among these was money or its equivalent. Respondents frequently felt it would be futile soliciting help of this type from relatives. The latter were often as hard pressed as they were and struggling to keep their own heads above water, e.g., 'My sisters couldn't help me—they got families of their own to keep.' A few respondents sought help which required specialized knowledge (assistance in budgeting, information about divorce procedures), while others sought help which reputedly required the authority of the worker (e.g. forestalling an eviction, interceding with creditors, help in getting better housing). Furnishing help of this type was felt to be beyond the province or competence of the informal network, which was accordingly by-passed.

Disclosures Would be Burdensome   Problems were sometimes concealed partially or entirely because their disclosure, it was felt, would prove burdensome to members of the network. Mrs Wrighton (a middle-class client) felt that her friends were providing her with useful help but she was imposing on them. 'I just talked to them and little things they said made me see things in a different way, and anyway, just by talking, suddenly an idea comes into your mind which is sparked off by something which somebody else says.' None the less, she went to the FWA, because she felt, among other reasons, that this process of clarifying things in her mind was taking up too much of her friends' time. On some occasions, disclosures may prove upsetting to the listener, or so the discloser believes. In this connection, one respondent stopped talking to a friend about a particular physical ailment which she and the friend had in common. These disclosures were allegedly making the friend apprehensive about her own condition.

If parents knew about the respondent's problems, they would purportedly worry—this was the principal reason why disclosures were visualized as burdensome. Mrs Small, for instance, was very concerned about her relationship with her husband, especially their financial troubles, but she felt that she could not tell her friends or her family about her difficulties. 'They knew a little about it, but not very much. It was not that I felt unable to trust them, but I just didn't want to worry them. As I remember, my brother was visiting from Australia at the time, and they were all excited at seeing him and I did not feel it was the right time to start telling them about my troubles. . . . I didn't want the family to know, particularly my mother. I feel she has had her life: she is very old and I did not want to worry her unduly.' Another wife remarked:

My mum's had a lot of worries and if I was to go around and tell her about my bills, she'd worry herself and try and get some money for me. I'm not saying that I didn't want it, but I couldn't expect it of her, because I knew she didn't have it. . . . Also I thought it wouldn't be fair, because she's got her own troubles. My mum knew the bill had come in, but I didn't let her think it was worryi ng me. (Mrs Sendall)

At a later point, Mrs Sendall mentioned why she preferred to confide in a social worker rather than her mother: 'When you go to the FWA, you don't feel that you're giving them your worries, because you know that when they go home they're not taking your worries with them.' These remarks illustrate how specific aspects of the interpersonal environment (fear of burdening others) may indirectly increase the attractiveness of professional services.

Untrustworthiness of Others   A number of respondents stated that they did not discuss their problems with members of their network, because the latter could not be trusted with confidences. Mrs Farrell reported that she did not tell her two close friends 'half what I told the women at the FWA. I knew my friends did not mix very much with the neighbours, but just in case what I might say got around, I said very little. . . . [On the other hand] I knew there would be no comeback from those women at the FWA.' The interviewee sometimes attributed this distrust of others to the fact that confidences had been violated in the past. Sometimes, however, their wariness derived from experiences of a more general sort. Mrs Lawton, for example, had heard her friends talking about other people and was determined not to be treated in the same manner. 'I know what women are,' she remarked, 'I've heard the way they talk about other people at times and I'm not going to be spoken about like that.'

One suspects that intimate communication within working class circles is greatly curbed by feelings of distrust such as those expressed. This possibility was suggested by an earlier study carried out by one of the authors (JM), which focused on a small group of working- and middle-class wives living in New York City. As many as one out of three of the working-class wives spontaneously voiced the opinion that other persons cannot be trusted with confidences, compared to one out of five of the middle-class wives.[6] We do not know how many of the FWA clients were similarly distrustful of others. However, it is significant that a number of these respondents tended to be especially impressed with the confidentiality of social work treatment. Many commented, sometimes with surprise, that what they had told the worker had gone no further, thus implying a contrast to what they were used to. Note, for example, the following comments, which once again illustrate how experiences with the informal network can affect one's reactions to professional help:

With a friend you can confide in them, but you don't know who else they're going to tell. But with these people, you know it's in complete confidence. You know that they're there talking to you and for you. (Mrs Brent)

What you are talking about with them doesn't go any further, because they're like doctors and lawyers. It's all confidential which helps a great deal. But with workmates or families you can talk to them and walk out of the room —then one of your brothers or sisters comes in and it's mentioned. (Mr West)

Cumulative Nature of Disclosures   Finally, there is a curious aspect associated with disclosing personal information: once an individual confides in another person, this very act may initiate a process leading to further disclosures—something which an individual may wish to avoid. For instance, Mrs Lawton said nothing about her marital troubles to her family, explaining, 'If I told my family *anything* about it, I would have had to tell them *all* about it and I did not really want to go on talking about it. They would want to know all that had happened and I would feel obliged to tell them.' Mrs Good's reasons for withholding her difficulties were somewhat similar. She felt that if she told her family anything about her difficulties, she might lose control and tell them all: 'I knew that once I started to tell them what had happened with the baby, I'd completely break down and tell them what my husband was like and what he was doing.' To avoid an unwanted train of circumstances in which 'one thing leads to another', both of these individuals said very little about their difficulties.

'Inadequate' responses of confidants

Some respondents, instead of concealing their difficulties from members of their network, disclosed them only to find the responses of their confidants inadequate in some way. The group we have already discussed tended to foresee certain problems connected with revealing their worries and thus remained silent; the group we are now concerned with tended, on the contrary, to try out their confidants, but with little success. The principal ways in which network responses were found to be inadequate will now be described.

Conflicting Advice   Sometimes the advice from different members of the network was conflicting—the informal network of friends and relatives is sometimes as unco-ordinated as the formal grouping of 'official' agencies. Mrs Clifford was caught up in a stressful relationship with her mother and husband—each was pulling her in an opposite direction. She talked to friends about this, but the talk produced only confusion. As Mrs Clifford explained, 'Each had their own theory, and sometimes I was more confused after talking to them than I was before. Sometimes one friend would tell me to try and make a go of it; she would say that things were not too bad. Then the other friend would say that she would leave her husband if he did to her what mine did to me, though a little later on she would say that he had probably been driven to it. . . . I didn't know what to think or do in the end.' Mrs Hunter was in a similar quandary. She had marital problems but was 'getting all different types of advice and didn't know what to do'. In the following, she describes the responses of her three closest friends:

> My friend, May, she would say to me, 'Try and bear up and take no notice. If he's going to have a good time, you have a good time. And don't worry about it. Just let him worry about it. Just leave it. Forget it completely.' And Joy would say, 'Oh, don't nag him. You're not going to leave him, so why talk about it.' Then Maureen would say, 'Leave him. Come down and stay with me. You know, bugger it. We'll go out and have a good time.'. . . I was getting to a desperate pitch and felt that maybe somebody more intelligent could sort it out for me.

As noted earlier, respondents were prepared in a sense to receive conflicting advice from different sides of the family and for this reason tended to keep their difficulties to themselves. There was less indication, however, that conflicting advice was expected from friends. Because it came as a surprise, it was probably especially disconcerting for respondents such as those cited.

Ineffective Advice   On some occasions it was felt that the confidant's advice, if followed, would simply prove ineffective— that is, that it would not solve the problem. Mr and Mrs Skinner, for example, had already tried out what their confidants were currently recommending. Specifically, they were very concerned over the behaviour of their sixteen-year-old daughter, who kept leaving various jobs, and staying out late without telling her parents where she was. The couple felt it might help if they sought help from others in the family. 'If there's just your husband and yourself, you can be talking about the same thing over and over again, both trying to puzzle out what to do. However, someone else may give you some idea of what to do.' The responses of relatives, however, turned out to be disappointing:

> They all suggested different things, which we had already done and which hadn't made any difference. Most of them said to me, 'Well, you want to keep her in', but I've done that time and time. I've kept her in for a month and as soon as the month was over, she would start again. . . . I even spoke to one of the governors that I was working under at the time. I didn't mind who I spoke to as long as I found a way, but I just couldn't.

To illustrate further, Mrs Mole felt that her husband needed to have 'some sense drummed into his head'. Accordingly, he was given a good 'talking-to' by Mrs Mole's sister, but to no avail. In view of the lack of results, the respondent felt that further efforts along these lines would be fruitless. Instead Mrs Mole went to the FWA, explaining, 'I thought somebody from outside, an authority of some kind, could talk some sense into him'.

Unacceptable Advice In some instances, the confidant's advice was considered 'sound', but other conditions led it to be viewed as untenable. For example, Mrs Carter was unwilling to follow her friend's suggestions (even though they might have worked), because they violated certain deeply held values or beliefs, specifically ones centering on 'marital equality'.

> Jenny said that instead of having a go at him when he comes in, for example, saying, 'Where do you think you've been this time of night', just ignore him, just let him sleep it off. 'Well', I said to her, 'why should he go out every other night and come home drunk and just sleep it off! I mean I'm his wife and I never get to go out!' . . . well, she

don't live with him, I do. So every time he come in, I said, 'Where do you think you've been!'

On one occasion, the solution proffered by the network would, in the eyes of the respondent, simply have created another problem. Mrs Norton talked with her family about the way in which her husband treated her. 'They said I was mad to stand it. They thought I should come back home to them. But that would have been no help, because there are six living in the house and it would have been murder living there.'

Withdrawal of Confidants   Finally, in some instances, the confidant or helper sought to disengage himself, at least according to the respondent's belief. Mrs Globe, who needed material assistance, sensed that both her mother and friend withdrew lest they be asked to help. In another case, a couple had a mutual friend who withdrew since it would allegedly be difficult for him not 'to go on one side or the other'. Other confidants were purportedly reluctant to make suggestions lest they turn out to be wrong. Still others, it is interesting to note, accompanied their withdrawal from the field with a recommendation that the client seek outside help. For example, Mrs Clifford was told by her friends that outsiders, since they are less 'prejudiced', are more apt to be helpful. Mrs Norton said of her mother and aunt, 'They told me that the FWA would help me out more than what they could, and what my mum says I always agree with. My mum said go, so I went.'

The reader will recognize that our treatment of the individual's communicative interaction with his network is greatly oversimplified. If we were to examine in detail any given individual's relationship with his confidants, we would very likely find a different constellation of processes operating at different points in time. In this connection, the distinction between 'choosing not to confide in others' and 'confiding in others but finding them inadequate' is not always a hard and fast one. True, these patterns may represent distinctive ways of dealing with different members of one's network. On the other hand, they may refer merely to different phases of an individual's interaction with the same person; for example, an individual may reveal a little about his problems to someone else, but finding the latter's response 'inadequate' may say no more in the future. In brief, the interactional situation is a complex one, and the categories employed represent merely a beginning attempt to order reality.[7]

There is a final matter that should be explicitly noted to avoid possible misunderstanding. The processes described should not be regarded as in any sense unique to persons seeking professional help. That is, there is a tendency for people in general to conceal their personal difficulties, to eschew the advice of others and so forth. We would suggest, however, that these processes are more marked in the case of those who *do* seek professional help, compared to those who do not. In other words, if we were to interview a group of troubled persons who were non-seekers of professional help we would expect to find that they had more confidants, communicated more openly with them, or found their responses more 'adequate' (or some combination of these). As a matter of fact, a recent study supports these expectations. Comparing the users of a family service agency in California with a random sample of families in the community, the authors found that clients had fewer friends and relatives living near by. Their ensuing suggestions are, in fact, very close to our own: 'It might be speculated that those individuals in the community who are somewhat more isolated would be more likely to turn to a formal agency for help when they need it . . . they might do so out of necessity because they have fewer friends and relatives to turn to for help when they experience personal problems.'[8] A similar interpretation is offered by the authors of another study. In seeking to explain why troubled persons with peripheral family statuses —e.g. the unmarried or those living apart from their families —make disproportionate use of public psychiatric facilities, the authors invoke the concept of 'credit networks'. They write: 'A person's credit network is determined by whom he can count on [for] how much help . . . when something goes wrong. People in aberrant or inadequate family structures have only sparse credit networks; therefore, in time of stress, these people appear in disproportionate numbers at public facilities.'[9]

A note on informal resources and treatment reactions

Our discussion has largely centred around the bearing that informal resources have for *establishing contact* with a professional agency. However, informal resources also affect what happens after contact; this is a convenient place to take note of one such inter-relationship.

The client's response to the casework situation will, to some extent, be a function of his earlier experiences with his informal network. One facet of this topic was already touched on in preceding illustrations: Clients were especially responsive to casework situations which in some way made up for 'deficiencies' in their network. For instance, respondents who were surrounded by 'gossipers' were especially appreciative of the confidential nature of casework treatment. Those who were surrounded by 'biased' persons were especially appreciative of its impartial nature. Another interconnection, even more important in our opinion, was suggested by our interview material. The client's reaction to the emotional support offered by the worker, it appears, was partially a function of how much support he received from his informal circle. Lack of data prevent us from exploring this generalization in any detail; it none the less deserves mention in view of its implications for treatment.

Specifically, the persons we interviewed can be roughly divided into two groups: 'non-communicators' and 'unsatisfied communicators'. The former comprise either those who were totally without confidants or those who, for one reason or another, chose not to utilize them. The unsatisfied communicators comprise those who made use of their confidants, but found them wanting in some way. Turning to the non-communicators, there are indications that they were especially responsive to the support offered by their workers. This seems perfectly reasonable in view of their earlier patterns of keeping things to themselves. For instance, it is not mysterious why clients like Mrs Watt experienced 'great relief' at the agency:

> I never used to tell nobody about my troubles. I just used to let it get me inside and then I couldn't stand it no more. .... Then all of a sudden it came on top of me. I went to the FWA and just broke down and told her everything.

The unsatisfied communicators, as noted earlier, often told us that their confidants failed to help them to solve their problems. But significantly, they often added that they received comfort and solace from them. While the support they received was not always stressed, it was, nonetheless, present as the following excerpts reveal:

I've found that telling people your problems don't help. It didn't help me any. Oh, at the spur of the moment, the talking and the getting it all off my chest for the minute I was there, I was all right. But it never solved my debt worry or arguments with my husband. (Mrs Hunter)

Talking to my friends was only helpful in that it tided me over. I got it off my chest—had a moan. I got a little bit of sympathy and a cup of tea. (Mrs Farrell)

One would expect that clients of this description, compared to non-communicators, would be in less need of emotional support from the worker. In this connection, one wife told us that she was very pleased that the worker was 'moderately' rather than 'terribly' sympathetic. When asked why, she explained, 'I didn't want him to be more sympathetic, because I got that from my parents.' Another wife commented that she derived no great satisfaction from being 'listened to' by the worker, because as she explained, 'I can do this with anybody— it doesn't have to be a welfare worker.'

These rather innocent, passing remarks are significant for several reasons. One, they bear on a question that social workers often wonder about: How much support need I offer this particular client? Or, framing the question in accord with issues raised in the introduction: under what conditions is it especially important that workers be 'warm' and supportive? The answer will presumably depend, in part, on the degree of warmth and support provided by the specific network of the client in question. Secondly, on a more general level, these remarks bear testimony to the inter-connection between informal resources and reactions to professional treatment. In doing this, they draw attention to an untapped area of research that calls for investigation.

4

The role of referral agents

In the preceding chapter we suggested that when the client viewed his problem solving resources as unsuitable or inadequate, he moved closer to seeking professional help. This fact in itself, however, leaves a number of questions unanswered. For one thing, it was not inevitable that the persons studied would seek professional help of any kind; they might have, instead, done nothing or taken to drink or spent more time praying. Moreover, even if they did consider professional help, it was not inevitable that they would go to the FWA; the Probation Service or the Marriage Guidance Council, among other agencies, represent viable alternatives. A complete analysis would try to account for the various choices made by the client and the turning points in the process. To repeat, why did these clients, faced with a breakdown or inadequacy in their problem-coping machinery, seek professional help *of any kind*? Furthermore, why did they select the FWA in particular? While these issues were of interest to us, they were not systematically explored in great depth which means that an analysis of the type outlined is precluded. Instead, we shall have to content ourselves with a more limited description of the processes involved.

To begin with, it is very clear that nearly all these clients were extremely distressed before coming to the agency. The problems which they brought to the agency were in no sense 'new'. By and large, they had been plagued with these difficulties for some time, generally about two years, and by the time they came to the FWA they felt themselves to be in serious difficulty. They repeatedly described how they were 'at their wits' end' and 'how desperate' they felt. Mrs Good's remarks below are typical. She had been having marital difficulties for some time and describes how she felt after learning of the latest episode—her husband's unfaithfulness:

> I was in a terrible state and walked the streets practically all night. It was raining and I was soaked to the skin. I remember that I came back to the flat, but I didn't go to bed. I just sat here and thought to myself, 'I must go somewhere and talk to somebody about this—I can't carry on like this.'

One might argue, of course, that these respondents were exaggerating their distress to emphasize the delinquency of the agency in not helping them more or in order to legitimize their own recourse to social work help: it is only desperation that makes it possible to assume the role of client with self-respect. Evidence from our interviews, however, suggests that the clients' distress was completely 'genuine'. First, many respondents referred to aspects of their concern that might be thought to carry a social stigma. Twenty-five referred in some way or other to the effect of their problem on their mental health. Some stated that they had had a breakdown or were afraid they would soon end up in a mental hospital or described how their problems led to drinking or incessant quarrelling. Some apparently contemplated suicide—'putting their head in the oven', 'taking an overdose of aspirin'—and several actually carried out acts of this type. It seems unlikely that acts and thoughts of this type would be invented for the interview occasion. Secondly, certain clients, notably those seeking material help, were dead-set against going to the agency, because of its implications of dependence and begging, which were often acknowledged.* The fact that they *did go* forcefully suggests in what desperate straits they felt themselves to be.

In brief, clients do not go to social work agencies unless they are sorely troubled, a fact revealed by other studies.[1] Still, distress in itself was not sufficient to account for why these individuals sought professional help and went specifically to the FWA. Certain other influences were also necessary, ones to which we shall now turn.

* These matters are discussed in Chapter 7.

Knowledge of the agency

Obviously, if persons are to go to a particular agency such as the FWA, they must be aware of its existence. Yet, shortly before their first contact, the large majority had never heard of the FWA. 'You don't see it advertised,' one individual remarked. 'If it were advertised, say in the welfare clinics, people in difficulties would know where to go, but they don't.' Only five respondents had any first-hand knowledge of the agency—three had been former clients and two knew of the agency's existence through their own observation. One woman, for example, happened to notice one day a small plaque on a building that said 'Family Welfare Association'. Several other clients had heard of the agency, but their imagery was typically vague and their information very partial.

How then did these persons learn of the agency's existence? About two thirds first learned of the FWA through official channels, primarily the Citizens' Advice Bureau and to a lesser extent the (then) NAB, child welfare clinics, probation offices and so on. The remaining one third became apprised through informal sources. Sometimes it was a relative who told the respondent about the FWA. Sometimes it was a friend, as in the case of Mrs Sendall:

> Before my husband went away [prison], we had a £21 electric light bill, and the baby needed clothes and it was near Christmas. I was in a state and didn't know what to do. A friend of mine had been to the FWA and she knew the trouble I was in and she told me to go there. . . . She had an electric light bill and a gas bill, so she went up there and they helped her out. She said how good they were and that it's worth your while going there.

Not infrequently, a stranger or acquaintance familiarized the client with the FWA. Mrs Globe related the following story:

> I just happened to be talking to this woman—she was just someone I used to speak with on the street. Anyway, I was saying something about the gas bill and I said, 'I don't know how I'm going to meet this bill—I just haven't the money and I'm afraid they're going to turn the gas off.' And she said to me, 'Oh, have you not tried the FWA?'

And I said, 'I'd never heard of it.' She advised me to go. She told me she had a lot of money stolen and that the FWA had met the bill.

It is interesting to note that clients were twice as likely to hear about the FWA through strangers and acquaintances as they were through friends. Perhaps this finding merely reflects the paucity of friends within the clients' social circles. However, it may derive from the possibility that friends are reluctant to admit having gone to the FWA for fear of losing face. Strangers and acquaintances, by contrast, may be less concerned with the client's opinion of them and for this reason may talk more freely. The plausibility of this interpretation is suggested by the following remarks. The client in question was not ashamed to tell a distant relative about his difficulties but would not have revealed them to someone closer. Below he recounts the circumstances leading him to the FWA:

> Now what put it into my head to go to the FWA was this friend. Well, he's not a friend—he's sort of a second or third cousin or something like that. Anyway, he's a lorry driver and we were sitting in this café one day, having a chat. I was feeling miserable, and I said that I owed some money. He doesn't enter my life really, he doesn't know me intimately or I would not have told him in the first place. He's just one of those that you say hello to, and that's that. Well, anyway, there we were talking, and he said did I know the welfare? He just happened to mention it. (Mr Dale)

It is worth noting that at a later point in the interview the client mentioned that his brother was having marital difficulties. The client was going to tell him about the FWA, but, significantly, on second thought reconsidered: he didn't want his brother to think that the FWA 'was footing his bills'.

If it is true that casual contacts play a large role in the referral process, this has at least one important implication. Casual contacts are not apt to be in continuous interaction with the person concerned and thus are not in a position to help the client over any sense of puzzlement in his initial, or perhaps later, contacts with the agency. On the other hand, friends are available, at least theoretically speaking; thus they are able to play an educative role and correct possible misunderstandings that emerge.

The 'push' of referral agents

The referral sources mentioned frequently did more than bring the FWA into the client's consciousness. In varying degrees, they pushed the client in the direction of the agency (that is, over and above the encouragement imparted by merely mentioning the agency, which presumably implies at least mild endorsement). Moreover, it is our impression that were it not for this 'push' certain clients (notably those seeking material assistance) would not have gone. In the following, the types of 'push' provided by formal and informal referral agents will be described.

Formal Agents Perhaps the major type of 'push' provided by formal agents arose through their taking the initiative in arranging contact. This occurred in about one-quarter of the cases. Typically, workers at the CAB or NAB contacted the FWA and arranged an appointment on behalf of the client. The importance of such procedures is suggested by the following:

> My husband went up to the CAB for advice. I don't know what they said to him, but the next couple of days he got a letter, which surprised him. They had made an appointment for him at the FWA. So he said to me, 'They've made an appointment—we'll go down and see them and see if they can help us.' He was quite pleased. (Mrs Norton)

Examples of this type were not confined to the CAB or NAB. Mrs Charles, for example, 'broke down' when she was in the hospital. The Sister said: 'Come and have a talk with me.' After seeing how distressed she was, the Sister arranged an appointment at the FWA.

Lack of data prevents us from discerning the precise role these procedures played. One would guess, however, that they eased the strain associated with making the first contact—the embarrassment and uncertainties—and at the same time placed the client under a mild commitment to follow through with any arrangements made. How many of these clients, if left 'on their own', would have gone to the agency must remain a moot point. However, the importance of such techniques is suggested by the findings of another study carried out in New York in 1953. It was found that 80 per cent of the clients 'followed through' on a referral when the referring agency took the initiative in establishing contact, as compared to only 40 per cent of those who were left 'on their own'.[2]

Easing the mechanics of contact was seemingly the major way in which 'push' was provided by official agencies. Sometimes, however, the client had established more than a passing relationship with the referrer and felt constrained to accept his referral suggestions. Mrs Small, for example, felt indebted to the child care officer who had been visiting her and was anxious not 'to let her down'. She described the situation below:

> I remember one day she came and she said that she had
> something to tell me: she hoped that I would not be cross.
> I said that I knew what it was, she was going to leave. She
> said that this was the case. She had been offered another
> job in another area with a lot more money. Well, what
> could I say? I could not say that she jolly well had to stay
> for my sake. Then she asked if I would do something for
> her sake. Would I meet somebody else, another worker
> from the welfare? It made me feel under an obligation. I
> felt that I must see this other person or else I would be
> letting her down. The lady from the Welfare came. She
> was very nice, but it somehow was not the same.

In some instances, one suspects that feelings of expediency played a role, that is, that the client was anxious not to cause offence. Mrs Wragg, for instance, had been in contact with the School Care Committee, who at a later date suggested she contact the FWA:

> I thought, well they [the School Care Committee] are
> trying to help me after all. I thought that perhaps if I
> refuse to see the FWA they will think that I am refusing
> help. I did not expect a great deal of response from the
> FWA, but I thought that if I said 'no' they would think
> I was a bit naughty.

Informal Agents We noted earlier that clients were sometimes alerted to the existence of the FWA by informal contacts who had themselves been clients. These various relatives, friends, acquaintances and strangers, however, did more than enlighten the client. They conveyed a very sanguine picture of the FWA which hastened the client's movement in that direction. These processes have already been illustrated incidentally, but merit further attention in view of their importance. Mrs Hunter, for example, told us that she was in 'terrible debt' due to her husband's gambling and 'couldn't stand the strain and worry of the debts' any longer. She relates how a chance encounter with a stranger gave her hope and drew her to the agency:

> I met a woman up at the laundry and I just was . . . oh, I was desperate! I just burst out crying. I thought I was on my own actually, it was late at night. And a woman started speaking to me, a complete stranger . . . I poured out my life to her. You know how you meet someone and you talk to them. She said that she'd been to the FWA and she knew others who had been there too. After telling her my case, she said that they were bound to help me— to give me financial help—that it was a dot on the cards. . . . And I thought to myself, well, I will go.

Sometimes, it appears, the informal contact merely recounted her experiences without going on to draw any implications this might have for the respondent. This, however, did not prevent the respondent from drawing her own conclusions. For instance, when Mrs Denton was asked what led her to the FWA, she replied:

> It was only through the woman next door telling me. She told me what it had done for her. She told me when she first came here they had some furniture in Hornsey Rise and they had no way of getting it over here. So the FWA gave her five pounds to get it over here. And I thought I'll see what I can get from them. I didn't mean it in a nasty way. It's just that I was desperate. And I thought they'd probably help me as well.

These various accounts by informal contacts were influential for several reasons. Not only did these individuals happen to have a very positive experience at the agency, but they tended to identify their particular experiences with the 'policy' of the 'welfare' as a whole. This is suggested by certain of the excerpts cited, but it is also a deduction from those respondents who, when asked about improvements in the agency that they would like to see, typically answered in terms of their own case or their own social worker. Thus, Mrs Charles, who was seen by a male worker, felt the agency should make an effort to employ female, as well as male, workers! The tendency to identify their own experience with 'agency policy' is perhaps not surprising in that clients are not apt to have other bases on which to form a judgment. It is unlikely, for example, that they will have any chance of seeing how the agency works with other clients. In any event, the end result of this process seems clear: certain clients in our group apparently felt their experiences would be a replication of those they heard about and in this sense they were 'pushed' towards the agency.

One might add at this point that formal referral agents did *not* apparently provide clients with an 'unrealistically' favourable picture of agency operations and to this extent imparted less 'push'. We gather, on the contrary, that their description of the agency was brief, vague, and matter-of-fact. While the client was encouraged to go to the FWA, nothing that was said would catapult him in that direction. The following excerpts are typical:

(Did the people at the court give you any idea what it would be like at the FWA?) Well, they just said that they'd come and see me if I wished. They would help me in any way they could. The magistrate said I needed somebody to come in and more or less talk things over and try to solve the problems one by one. (Mrs Brain)

(What did the Probation Officer tell you about the FWA?) She didn't say much, she just told me where they were. She told me that they were the people I should see to help me—you know, that they would advise me and tell me what to do. (Mrs Stanton)[3]

There is a further reason why informal reports of experience were influential in leading clients to the agency. Clients, it will be recalled, knew very little about the agency before going; in the typical case, they knew nothing aside from what they gleaned from the informal contact. The absence of other informational sources heightened the impact of the one source at their disposal. This so-called 'contextual vacuum' made whatever they heard stand out more starkly and prevented them from checking up on its accuracy. One wonders what would have happened if our respondents had encountered ex-clients whose experiences had been unfavourable. One suspects that they never would have gone to the FWA (and thus become part of a research enterprise such as this.)[4]

Finally, one other way in which informal referral agents promoted contact with the agency should be mentioned. Occasionally a member of the immediate family—a spouse or parent—was in contact with the agency, and pressure was subsequently placed on the respondent to follow suit. Generally the respondent went in order to satisfy the requests of the family member and/or the agency, although one wife allegedly went in order to 'put her case'—to let her husband and the agency know that she had nothing to hide.

The material presented in this chapter suggests that referral agents played an important role in leading certain individuals to the FWA. At the same time it will be recognized that the steps leading an individual from his informal milieu to the door of a professional helper may be a good deal more complex than we have made out. For example, some persons moved through referral chains of various types before arriving at the agency. One person moved from the NAB to a solicitor to the CAB and finally the FWA; another moved from a relative to a medical social worker and then to the FWA. Such chains might usefully be looked at in terms of the number of referral agents involved, their statuses (whether formal or informal), the relative influence of the various links and so forth.[5]

Before closing, let us return once more to the types of 'push' described in this chapter. If we compare the primary way in which informal and formal agents fostered contact, we emerge with the following: informal agents fostered contact by providing the respondent with a very selective picture of the agency's operations—one which would lead him to believe that his needs, as he saw them, would in all likelihood be met. Formal agents, on the other hand, fostered contact not in this way, but by easing the mechanics of contact—that is, by taking the initiative in arranging the first meeting, thereby relieving the client of possible strain and perhaps placing him under some obligation.

Each of these mechanisms appears to be an effective device for inducing contact. The former (the selective picture type) however, raises certain questions. Respondents who have high hopes of receiving help (and this typically meant material help) may be sorely disappointed if their wishes are not fulfilled. This, as a matter of fact, is exactly what happened in the case of two clients earlier cited (Mrs Hunter and Mrs Denton). Neither received any material assistance, and each incidentally recognized that her disappointment was a function of her earlier expectations. This suggests that agencies that selectively offer material assistance should perhaps caution 'successful' clients that not everyone receives help of this type. But this, too, has its drawbacks, for, in partially dampening the enthusiasm of such clients, the latter are less apt to act as envoys and so refer those who might profit by the experience. How this dilemma might best be handled merits further thought.

Clients seeking help with interpersonal problems

5

Dissatisfied clients

In this chapter we shall deal with some of the processes leading clients in search of 'interpersonal' help to feel dissatisfied.* Specifically, we will describe what they expected treatment to be like, their reactions to the services actually offered, and their attempts to explain or 'make sense' of what was happening. After that, an effort will be made to re-examine, in more general terms, why a breakdown in the helping process occurred.

First, however, a few preliminary words. To begin with, when these clients (as well as satisfied ones) first came to the agency, they did not have precise, explicit expectations as to what would happen. They were uncertain about many aspects of the situation, e.g., what the worker would be like, how many meetings there would be, where they would be held and so forth. This is hardly surprising, since, as we have seen, few had previously been to the FWA (or a comparable agency) and not a great many more knew people who had or at least talked about it. This haziness in expectations may be typical of family agency clients in general. For example, the authors of another study who interviewed such clients in California, remark: '. . . it is apparent that there is no popular imagery of Family Service Agencies comparable to the rather clear-cut (even if not wholly accurate) imagery of what to expect from more conventional services such as those rendered by doctors, psychiatrists, lawyers, ministers and even marriage counsellors'.[1] However, on a more fundamental and typically implicit level,

* Large sections of this chapter are reprinted from *Social Casework*, Vol. 50, No. 1, January 1969 by permission of Family Service Association of America.

the clients we interviewed (particularly dissatisfied ones) very definitely *did* have expectations; they had basic preconceptions concerning the ways in which workers would deal with their difficulties—something which will become evident as we proceed.

Secondly, what about the social workers who treated these dissatisfied clients seeking interpersonal help? While it is clear that their treatment approach differed substantially from that of other workers to be discussed later, we cannot provide a detailed picture of what they were doing. Many of them were not interviewed and those who were sometimes found it difficult to talk in detail about their treatment plans and methods of working. However, from the material available, plus the reports of clients and talks with supervisory personnel at the FWA, it is possible to construct a reasonably accurate picture of what they were attempting to do. By and large, they were trying to give the client a better understanding of his problems, primarily by revealing how he himself was contributing to them. Using the phrase loosely, they were trying to provide the client with some psychological insight into his difficulties, in short to increase his 'self-understanding' or 'self-awareness'. Much of the time, particularly in the beginning, was spent listening to the client. Later on, they increasingly drew the client out along certain lines and in many instances the lines they followed required the client to shift the focus of his attention.

The clients' expectations

In coming to the agency, these dissatisfied clients seeking interpersonal help expected the worker to listen to their stories and then, after one or possibly two sessions, to reach a conclusion based on the 'rights' and 'wrongs' of the situation. Mrs Lawton, for example, who felt wronged by her husband, did not know whether it was proper for her to leave him because of her obligations to her children. She fully expected the worker to point out the right course to follow. Other wives—and this refers to those who, at the moment, had no thought of leaving their husbands—expected the worker, after learning of their marital troubles, to arrive at a moral assessment. For example, Mrs Lennon, after describing how she treated her husband, remarked, 'I thought they'd tell me whether I was doing right or whether I was doing wrong.'

The clients' anticipation of such judgments does not necessarily imply that *they* had any doubt about who was right and who was wrong. Typically they thought they were right, and they fully expected the worker to agree with them. Despite a belief in their rightness, these clients, none the less, appear to have made special efforts to present their cases in a dispassionate and balanced manner. Presumably they did so because they believed it was the correct way to act in the presence of a judge —the outside authority who renders an impartial decision. Furthermore, they may have thought that it was in their interest to present themselves as reasonable, just, tolerant persons so that their allegations would appear more credible.

It is significant that the clients did not usually expect the worker's activity to end simply with the making of a moral assessment. On the contrary, they fully expected the worker also to assist in rectifying the situation by helping them to implement his decisions. The clients took it for granted that the only way to improve the situation was to bring about changes in the offender's behaviour. They anticipated help from the social worker in this direction. He could, for example, instruct the client in ways of acting that would lead the culprit to behave differently. Expectations of this nature were clearly held by Mrs Farrell, who stated:

> I can easily tell you what I thought it would be like going to the agency. I would bare my soul and my reactions to what my husband did and said. I would hold nothing back, like I do with the neighbours. I would tell the lady all the nasty things that I did back to Brian, and I thought she would say, 'If you didn't say this or react like that, Brian wouldn't react like he does.' As for Brian, I was hoping that they would tell him, 'Well, if you didn't treat Mary like that, she wouldn't lose her temper and scream and go into hysterics.' It would have helped build something out of the marriage if the woman had said, 'You shouldn't have said that' or 'You shouldn't have done that' or 'I think your marriage would work if you didn't do that, Mary, or if you didn't do that, Brian.'

Most clients hoped that the worker, instead of merely prompting them from the wings, so to speak, would deal directly with the 'offender' himself. For instance, the worker might hopefully draw the husband himself into treatment and make him 'see the way things were' and, if necessary, 'drum some sense into his head'. Or, if warranted, the worker might insist that the husband see a psychiatrist. Or he might possibly bring more coercive measures to bear. For instance, Mrs Kent, whose husband was depleting the family's resources by gambling, thought the FWA should have sent an 'inspector' to see him. 'He could have come to see my husband,' she said, 'and put pressure on him. He could have put the case that he was neglecting his children and me and that he would have to do something about it.'

These working-class clients apparently spent little time trying to ferret out the causes of their problems, unlike persons of middle-class background who see many causal possibilities and who believe it is essential to identify the correct ones. To these particular clients, the cause of the trouble was obvious—it was the other person. The paramount task, therefore, was not to unearth causes, but to find effective ways of reforming the offender, which usually meant deterring him from acting in objectionable ways. This way of coping with problems was in no sense novel to these clients. Before coming to the agency, they typically had dealt with personal problems by bringing pressure to bear on the other person whenever possible. The fact that they had sought professional help in no sense implied a loss of faith in their techniques. Rather, they had sought professional help because they hoped the caseworker would prove to be more effective in wielding essentially the same techniques.

The description which Gerald Sanctuary gives of clients who go to the Marriage Guidance Council in many ways parallels the one we have just given:

> Most clients expect to be given some kind of answer to their problem. They imagine that the counsellor will listen to them, then sum up the problem, give appropriate advice or instruction and send them away to try it out. It is not uncommon for a client to tell the story and then sit back, folding her arms, saying, 'Well, you're the expert. What ought I to do?'

And at another point in the account:

> When clients first come to see a counsellor ... they almost always
> have a complaint to make about the way their partner
> is behaving. At first they usually blame their partner;
> in fact, when clients first start the interview by blaming
> themselves it is often because they are cloaking their own
> resentment against their partner, or because they want to
> enlist the sympathy of the counsellor. During counselling,
> clients very frequently try to manipulate the counsellor
> into taking action for them. Others expect the counsellor
> to persuade their partner to change his behaviour.[2]

The clients' reactions

The clients in this group reacted, at least initially, to the
workers' insight-oriented approaches with surprise and puzzlement. They were bewildered by certain aspects of the workers'
behaviour. For one thing, they frequently commented on their
lack of active participation. The following comment typifies
the clients' attitude:

> The welfare lady came to the house one day when my
> husband was home and there was a big row between us. I got
> up to it with my husband and he got up to it with me.
> The welfare lady knew very well what I went through with
> my husband, but she just sat there and listened, and she
> never tried to do anything. She just listened and didn't
> drum any sense into my husband at all. (Mrs Carter)

Mrs Lawton, who had expected concrete advice from the
social worker, told the research interviewer:

> I thought the welfare worker was going to give me some
> advice as to whether to stay with my husband or leave him.
> But she didn't give me any advice at all. I think she
> expected me to keep coming back and by talking it out I
> would get over it and everything would be back to normal
> at home. You know what I mean? She gave me the
> impression that by talking to somebody, all my troubles
> would disappear. Because she kept wanting me to come
> back, that was the idea.

When she was asked to relate the kinds of things she had talked about with the worker, Mrs Lawton said:

The social worker asked me what went wrong and I told her. She asked me why does my husband act like he does, and what sort of things does he say. And I was giving her the answers, but she wasn't giving me anything back. Then she would ask me another question. She kept asking me questions, and I would be giving her the answers. I would expect somebody to say, 'Well, why don't you do this?' or 'Why don't you do that?'

It is interesting to note that Mrs Lawton's expectations stemmed in part from earlier experiences at another social work agency. In her opinion, the worker there really knew the 'answers':

The lady there really gave me the reasons why my husband was acting the way he was . . . I remember she said, 'I think you should leave him, because by the sound of this, this type of person doesn't change. From what you have told me, your husband sounds psychopathic.' She said, 'It's no good you hanging on there, because it won't be any different. The best thing you can do is to save up and get some money and go.' And really I felt she knew what she was talking about—much more than the one at the FWA. She had faced this type of situation before and met people like my husband.*

The non-activist approach of the workers and their emphasis on talk was not the only thing that surprised and puzzled the clients. Frequently they were taken aback by the workers' tendency to focus on *them* rather than the person they thought was responsible for the difficulty. Mr and Mrs Skinner, for example, had been very concerned because their sixteen-year-old daughter often left jobs and stayed out late at night and did not tell her parents where she was. The parents finally turned to the agency in the hope that someone would get through to Penny and make her realize how silly she had been. It is evident from Mrs Skinner's report of her experiences that

* For a discussion of the general relevance of previous helpers see Appendix 2.

the worker viewed the problem as related more to the parents than to the daughter.

> The social worker wanted to know all about our background when we were young and all that, and I said to my husband, 'Well, to my opinion, that's nothing to do with it.' The social worker just talked about us most of the time, instead of trying to get to the bottom of the problem. When we told . . . [relatives] what had happened they said, 'It don't seem right. It's you that's undergoing the treatment, not Penny.'

After their fourth interview Mr and Mrs Skinner dropped out. Mrs Skinner gave the following explanation:

> When we came out of there the fourth time, my husband said, 'What do you think of it?' and I said, 'I don't know what to think of it.' Then my husband said, 'He just don't give you any idea what he's going to do or anything. He just keeps on saying come back and have some more talks and he says he's going to have more talks and more talks. Well, while he's doing that, we're not getting anywhere. Penny's the problem, not us.'

Like other clients we interviewed, Mr and Mrs Skinner did not press the worker for an explanation of his activities. Their reticence was partially (though not wholly) due to their perception of the client role. They were dealing with 'an expert' and it would be presumptuous to challenge his 'expertise'.[3]

The tendency of practitioners to probe into the past was seen as still another puzzling aspect of their approach. Mrs Carter thought such activities had little to do with solving her problems. When the research interviewer asked why the social worker delved into her background, Mrs Carter replied:

> Well, she was trying to be helpful, but she wasn't. She was more like a person that was going into you mentally. I can't explain it. She kept asking me about my background and all that—about things that were bothering me when I was a young girl. But that's got nothing to do with what's going on now. Well, that wasn't going to solve my problems, was it? I mean, it's now. I'm grown up now.

The clients' explanations of why their workers were exploring the past reveal a variety of misconceptions. Mrs Hastings stated that the worker was trying to 'take the pressure off'. She was convinced the worker was shifting the focus away from her current difficulties with her husband to a more pleasant topic in order to relax her and provide a quieting interlude. Another client, Mrs Page, assumed that the purpose of the questions was to learn how deserving she was: once the worker learned how difficult her life had been, he would understandably be more anxious to help. She said it was a good idea for social workers to ask about the client's background, because 'they sort of know where they stand before they begin asking you about your troubles'.

It is worth noting that workers and clients were seemingly in agreement on at least one point. As a rule, both were very much in favour of other parties to the difficulty being drawn into treatment (generally a spouse, but sometimes a child). If one looks closer, however, it is apparent that they had entirely different reasons for favouring this course. Some wives, for example, felt that if their husbands became involved the worker would then be able to see first-hand exactly what they (the wives) had to contend with. Significantly, the worker would then be in a position to 'straighten him out', perhaps by giving him a 'good talking-to'. Several felt that without the husband's participation, there was little point in continuing. For example, Mrs Bedford, who had earlier dropped out of treatment, remained certain that nothing could be done 'unless my husband goes in and sees what they say about him'.

Clients not only stressed the importance of joint participation in general, but felt in particular that the two parties should be seen at the same time by the same worker. For example, Mrs Norton (a satisfied client to whom we shall return later) felt that if the two were seen together her husband would no longer be able to turn a deaf ear to her complaints, as he had in the past, either by ignoring her, walking out, or telling her to 'shut up'. In the presence of an 'authoritarian' outsider, he would have to listen to her for once in his life. Other clients remarked that joint sessions would enable them to correct the inevitable lies their husbands would tell and would prevent their husbands from misrepresenting, at a later time, what the worker had told them about their conduct.

The clients' explanations

Understandably the clients tried to make sense of the treatment situation. They tried to find reasons for the strange and totally unfamiliar actions of the social workers. Several different reasons were offered in explanation of their behaviour.

Some clients reasoned that their workers were simply not interested in them and therefore not overly anxious to help them. Mrs Lawton came to this conclusion, remarking:

> Once I got talking to the social worker, I felt at ease, but then I realized that she wasn't entering into what I was saying at all. And I thought, You are not really listening to me. You are not really interested. She just wasn't giving me an answer or any advice at all. . . . She just kept saying, 'Yes, yes' in a quiet sort of way and nodding her head and would I like to come back and that sort of thing.

Other clients concluded that the workers did not understand their difficulties and therefore failed to deal with the problems effectively. Mrs Kent, for example, thought the worker did not really grasp the terrible effect of her husband's gambling on the family. Mrs East, whose husband evidenced symptoms of mental illness, commented, 'No matter how I put it, I felt she didn't understand what it was like to live with a man like my husband.'

It should be added that the caseworkers were not necessarily blamed for their inability to understand. The clients assumed that only persons who had had a similar experience could possibly comprehend what it was like. This assumption incidentally explains one of our findings—namely, that clients typically preferred workers of the same age, marital status, and sex as themselves. Being similar, they would understand what they, the clients, had been through. One might further add that this assumption challenges a fundamental precept of the social work professi on earliernoted, namely, that social work skills derive from a body of abstract knowledge. The belief that workers must actually *live through* certain situations and events, if they are to be helpful, is an implicit challenge to this axiom.

Several clients assumed that the workers distrusted the

authenticity of their stories and for this reason failed to take any action. One such client, Mrs Crew, told the interviewer:

> I was disappointed when the social worker remarked, 'We don't give advice as you notice. Also I don't really know you.' Which of course she did not, to be fair—as it was the first time I had come in. But with the training that I understand these welfare officers have, they must be a pretty good judge of character whether anyone is telling the truth or not . . . the point is I personally can judge whether I would trust a person or not . . . if you came to me with problems I would listen to your problem and if I felt it was genuine and quite honest, I would give an advice there and then as to what should be done.

Like Mrs Crew, Mr West felt that it does not take long 'to sum a person up', especially for social workers in view of their experience.

> If you are talking to someone you can usually tell what his background is by what he says and the way he dresses. And it doesn't really take very long, especially for welfare people—they meet so many people . . . so many different classes of people that they can talk to someone, say for a few hours, and they can then read them like a book.

Since Mr West's social worker failed to take 'appropriate' action, he concluded that in the eyes of the worker there was something spurious about him or his grievances. In other words, had the workers involved in these two cases been more trusting, allegedly they would have 'done' something.

Several clients were of the opinion that, because of the conflicting stories of the client and his spouse, the workers did not know how to proceed and therefore did nothing. Mrs Carter stated, 'The social worker listened to my husband's side and to mine, but she just didn't come to a decision about what to do. She just couldn't tell who was right and who was wrong.' Mrs Mole remarked that she had no idea what the social worker thought about her problem, since the latter 'didn't say one way or the other'. When asked why the worker was non-committal, Mrs Mole replied, 'Well, I suppose the poor woman didn't really know which side to take. Did she now? I mean, since me and my husband were both going up there, I suppose she couldn't decide her favourite side to take.'

Finally, in the opinion of some clients, lack of authority prevented the worker from acting in a 'reasonable' manner. The clients recognized in varying degrees that the authority of a social worker was limited. They knew, for example, that a social worker could not insist that a husband come to the agency, or force a husband to relinquish his wages to his wife. Significantly, these clients tended to believe that the worker would employ such measures if given the opportunity. In other words they tended to believe that they and the worker were in essential agreement concerning how the case should be handled from an ideal point of view.

The reasons clients gave for the workers' failure to act in a so-called appropriate manner are of interest. They strongly suggest that the clients were almost totally unaware that the workers' approach to problem-solving was fundamentally different from their own. The clients tacitly assumed that the workers shared their approach. They, therefore, proceeded to find special reasons why the workers' actions had not been guided by it. In other words, the clients attributed their own cultural perspective to their caseworkers, in much the same way that persons of middle-class background occasionally attribute their perspective to working-class persons. This process is clearly illustrated by the remarks of one of the clients, who was disturbed because the worker had not advised her about leaving her husband. Significantly, she had not told the worker that she wanted such advice.[3] The research interviewer asked why she had not, and the client replied, 'Because I thought she'd *know* what to do. I just thought it would come natural to her to know how to help me.'

It would appear that the 'explanations' we have depicted played an important part in influencing the clients to drop out. The clients who felt that the worker was not interested in them or did not trust them became angry and resentful—and in developing such feelings moved closer to terminating contact. The clients who concluded that the worker did not understand, was confused, or lacked authority seemed to resign themselves to the fact that the workers would be unable to help. There was little point, therefore, in continuing treatment.[4]

A clash in perspective

To review briefly, these particular clients had a distinctive way of conceptualizing and coping with interpersonal problems. They were not oriented to exploring causes, particularly the possibility that they were contributing in some way to the difficulty under discussion. As they saw it, the cause of the problem was obvious—it arose from the 'blameworthy' actions of the other person. Moreover, if the situation was to be improved, changes would have to be brought about in the 'culprit's' behaviour and this could be accomplished, as a rule, only through deterrent action of some kind.

Significantly, these clients assumed that their workers would share their general outlook and would act accordingly. When it turned out that their workers did not act as expected, the clients found special reasons to account for their 'delinquency': The worker was 'not interested' in them, he was 'confused', he was powerless to do anything, etc. These clients did not discern that the practitioner's behaviour—his shifting the focus of attention, his passivity, etc.—sprang from a different set of assumptions about behaviour and its possible modification.[5]

These findings are congruent with, yet go beyond, previous studies concerned with the reactions of working-class persons to psychotherapy. It has been stated that members of the working-class do not understand psychotherapeutic processes; that they attribute personal difficulties to external conditions; that they expect the therapist to give advice and take an active role; and that they lack the conceptual and linguistic skills to maintain themselves in a psychotherapeutic encounter.[6] Many of these findings were also confirmed in the present study. However, the fact that we interviewed clients enabled us to suggest that the so-called 'inadequacies' or 'deficiencies' in the thinking of working-class people, when it comes to solving problems, are actually by-products or derivatives of a *different system* of problem-solving—one that begins from different premises. In other words, the behaviour of these clients, when viewed in its proper context and not by middle-class standards, becomes more understandable and consistent. Benjamin Paul's remarks about using one cultural system as a basis for describing another are pertinent at this point. 'One system . . . seems to dissolve or fragment the second system, so that the other group's ways of behaving and thinking appear as an illogical patchwork.'[7]

It is our impression that the social workers were unaware that the clients entered the treatment situation with a different mode of problem-solving and that the clients' behaviour during treatment was in part traceable to this fact. In the research interviews with the workers, the client's behaviour was interpreted by the workers largely, and sometimes nearly exclusively, in psychodynamic terms. The workers consistently viewed discontinuance as stemming from anxieties aroused by treatment: in other words, the clients could not look at the ways in which they were contributing to the problem.

There is almost a Kafkaesque quality about these worker-client interactions. To exaggerate only slightly, each of the parties assumed that the other shared certain of his underlying conceptions about behaviour and the ways in which it might be altered. Then, unaware of the inappropriateness of his extrapolations, each found special reasons to account for the other's conduct. In saying this, we are not implying that the workers involved in these cases were necessarily wrong in attributing a reluctance on the part of the client to recognize his role in the difficulty. Resistances of this type may have been present. However, it is abundantly clear that other elements were *also* involved, ones which must be taken into account in interpreting the reactions of clients. (For a discussion of the non-assimilation of professional norms as an additional barrier between worker and client see Appendix 3.)

It is worth stressing once again that the situation under review does not involve *merely* a difference in outlook between two actors. It is one in which the differences are unrecognized. In this sense it departs from other interpersonal encounters. For example, in a dating situation, the male may be interested in seduction and that alone, while his partner has her heart set on marriage. However, unlike the worker-client interactions described, each is apt to be *aware* of the other's viewpoint and interests.

Lack of data prevent us from knowing how typical the working-class problem-solving approach depicted is of working-class people in general. Certainly, it is not characteristic of *all* working-class members, at least to the same extent. This will become evident as we proceed. Moreover, not all middle-class members, for their part, are cut from the same cloth; some will undoubtedly have views that are similar to those we have described. Despite variations, there are, none the less, grounds—both empirical and theoretical—for expecting to find a uni-causal-moralistic-suppressive approach (to use an accurate but cumbersome phrase) more prevalent within working-class circles.

Previous research focusing on differences between a small group of working-class and middle-class wives in New York[8] supports this conclusion, as do the studies of Mirra Komarovsky and others.[9] Moreover, the clients' orientation fits in well with other aspects found to be part of the culture of the working class.[10] It has been frequently observed that working-class persons, compared with middle-class persons, are more oriented to the present. Such an outlook seems to be especially compatible with an approach to problem-solving that relies on deterrence, in contrast to one that seeks to uncover underlying causes and to effect changes in them. The latter approach may seem more appropriate to persons seeking long-term changes, that is, alterations in behaviour that have staying power and continue to be effective in the future. However, if one is primarily interested in the present—and thus more concerned with producing short-run changes—coercive measures may well prove 'effective'. That is, they may work in the sense of curbing the offensive behaviour, and their appeal may be enhanced through a failure to recognize that behaviour is interrelated—in other words, that such procedures may produce dysfunctional consequences in other areas of the partners' interaction. Moreover, because such deterrent measures are relatively easy to understand and simple to invoke, they fit in well with the working-class person's preference for the 'least complex alternative', a working-class trait pointed out by Seymour Lipset in his discussion of working-class authoritarianism.[11]

The use of deterrent measures may also stem from the view that the causes of behaviour are not subject to modification (which in turn may derive from the working-class person's sense of powerlessness—a theme frequently commented upon in the literature).[12] In this connection, Komarovsky notes that the 'why' of behaviour was not explored by the working-class persons she interviewed. Instead, 'explanations fall back upon moral weakness, inherited traits or individual idiosyncrasy'.[13] In another study, also based on interviews, the author concludes that lower class persons, in contrast to those of upper-middle class background, are 'inclined to explain . . . behaviour as a fundamentally immutable aspect of personal character rather than something that could be manipulated or changed by insight or counselling'.[14] In our view, beliefs of this type generate a dependence on deterrent measures. For example, if a husband gambles, what can his wife do but bring pressure to bear? True, she might become resigned or leave him, but if she wishes to change his behaviour her options are limited. By contrast, her counterpart in the middle-class, having a multi-causal view of behaviour, may switch to another tactic should her current problem coping efforts fail. It would appear, in other words, that conceptions of behavioural causality generate corrective measures of a certain type.[15]

Finally, the working-class perspective described seems not to be confined to problem-solving on a personal level. Seemingly it is representative of a generalized response to deviant behaviour. Evidence suggests that working-class persons are more apt to favour repressive measures in dealing with criminals, drug addicts, and mentally ill persons or in coping with such phenomena as race riots and insurrections. On the other hand, middle-class persons, at least in comparison with members of the working class, are more inclined to favour a rehabilitative approach. They tend to be more concerned with causes and in effecting changes in these, rather than applying pressure as a means of curbing deviant behaviour.[16] In sum, there are a number of reasons why one would expect to find a unicausal-moralistic-suppressive approach more characteristic of working-class persons.

At a later point, we will consider some of the implications of an insight-oriented approach for working-class persons of the kind described. However, a few preliminary words may be appropriate now. While this approach was not successful with the particular clients studied, one should not flatly conclude that *ipso facto* it has no value, especially on the basis of the small number of cases studied. A more appropriate question is, 'under what conditions might it be successful?' We should add that the social workers dealing with these particular clients did very little to familiarize them with the suppositions underlying their treatment approach, and this raises questions about the possibilities of 'resocializing' clients of this description. In brief, is it possible to 're-educate' such clients to the views of insight-oriented practitioners? Personally we are somewhat sceptical in view of the ingrained (or cultural) nature of the clients' thinking. However, questions of the type raised are best postponed until other cases in our group have been surveyed.[17]

6

Satisfied clients

In this chapter, the focus remains on clients who sought help in dealing with someone else in their environment, but we shall consider those who were satisfied with the services received. In trying to account for their positive reaction—which is the object of this chapter—one fact immediately stands out. These particular clients were *not* caught up in the kinds of misunderstandings which we have already depicted. They did not infer, for example, that their social workers were uninterested in them or distrusted them; nor did they misconstrue the purpose of the various treatment techniques employed.

Yet, it is clear that the absence of misunderstanding does not in itself ensure client satisfaction. As a matter of fact, some of our clients did know what their workers were about, but remained dissatisfied nonetheless. For example, in one instance the worker was trying to effect a reconciliation between the husband and wife, but this was not what the client wanted, and the worker's efforts were resented. In brief, understanding on the part of the client is important but it is not always enough to ensure satisfaction. What else is necessary?

In an attempt to deal with this broad and multi-faceted question, we extracted all remarks from the clients' interviews which had a bearing, direct or otherwise, on the reasons for their satisfaction. We found that they could be adequately grouped (with exceptions to be noted later) under the following headings: relief from unburdening; emotional support; enlightenment; and guidance. These categories, it will be noted, closely parallel those developed by Florence Hollis in her useful classification of treatment procedures: ventilation (relief through unburdening); sustaining procedures (emotional support); reflective processes (enlightenment); and procedures of direct influence (guidance).[1] The main difference between the two classifications (aside from the greater internal differentiation of the Hollis scheme) is one of perspective. The Hollis scheme describes the activities or communications of workers irrespective of their impact on the client; our scheme, on the other hand, is undertaken from the standpoint of clients and intentionally registers their reactions (which happen to be positive in this instance) to the various transactions of treatment. The difference in perspective is reflected in the choice of words used to describe the main categories.

In the following, the comments of satisfied clients will be discussed under our headings already mentioned. It need hardly be added that because clients were satisfied in one way does not mean that they were not also satisfied in other ways. Casework is an admixture of various procedures, and clients who receive 'emotional support', for example, may also receive 'enlightenment' as well. In other words, the compartmentalization required by exposition fails to provide a complete picture of what happened in any given case.

Reasons for satisfaction

Relief through unburdening

According to their testimony, satisfied clients seeking interpersonal help received considerable relief by unburdening themselves to the worker.[2] Because they felt at ease with the worker, they were able to talk freely; and because they talked freely, their tensions were eased, at least temporarily.

> The first time I went, I was there for two hours and I didn't stop talking once. It was marvellous and I felt very much better when I left. I was a completely different person. (Miss Bell)

> I just felt like I was talking to an old friend and just pouring out my troubles. She heard all I've got to say and out it goes. (Mrs Mole)

On some occasions, the clients had kept things pretty much to themselves in the past. When this was the case, they were apt to receive even more relief in unburdening, as for example, Mrs Wragg: 'I felt as if I'd lifted a load off when I first went, because I'd bottled it all up inside me.' In some instances, difficulties had been bottled up seemingly as a matter of principle, e.g., 'I've always kept problems to myself, until I couldn't stick it any longer.' Sometimes it seems to have been more a matter of disposition: 'I'm not one for shouting and having an argument. I'm afraid I sort of bottle it up inside me, rather than rant and rave.' On other occasions, clients were eager to disclose their problems but unfortunately lacked confidants, e.g., 'I've always wanted someone I could talk to, ever since my parents died when I was eighteen.' Whatever the reasons for the reticence of these clients, once the dam was broken, the flood could hardly be stopped. It is worth noting that the fact of unburdening was sometimes taken by the social worker as an indication that the clients *understood* the social worker's activity in this beginning phase of the contact.

The relief experienced by these clients did not derive solely from their access to a sympathetic listener; nor even to their having previously 'bottled up' their difficulties. To some extent their relief was also a by-product of former experiences with welfare personnel of one type or another. In previous encounters with doctors, NAB (as they were then) officials and others, the clients had often felt hurried. The fact that this was *not* so at the FWA gave them additional comfort. Mrs Globe, for instance, always felt she was 'pestering' her doctor because 'they haven't really got the time to listen to you. But the man at the FWA always seemed to have time to sit and listen to you.' Feelings of hurriedness in dealing with welfare personnel certainly have a basis in reality. General practitioners, for example, are unable to allot as much time to applicants for service as are social workers at the FWA. But matters of attitude also seem to be involved. Research findings from the U.S. suggest that working-class people are apt to feel they are imposing on a doctor if they take up too much of his time; compared to those with more education, income or better jobs, they were more likely to agree with the statement: 'I don't like to bother the doctor unless it's necessary.'[3] Perhaps the working-class persons we interviewed also had attitudes of this type and for this reason especially appreciated the unhurried, patient approach of the FWA workers.

Emotional Support   Clients were not only given a chance to talk about their problems to a sympathetic audience—they were also buoyed up or actively supported in various ways by the worker. The importance of this process can be gleaned from the following excerpts:

> *Mrs Clifford*: Going there made me feel better. It sort of made me feel more light-hearted when I left after those talks. I sort of felt, well somebody understands and they're interested and they want to help and they don't think it's silly.

> *Mrs South*: The social worker was nice and pleasant and very polite and quiet in his ways. And sort of steady in asking the questions. The second time I went I felt a bit better in myself and the third time I felt even stronger. Each time I was able to tell him more of what happened. I felt as though he was giving me great strength, that I had someone behind me. I felt that if anything really went wrong, that I had him to go to.

> *Mrs Royal* (who had fallen in love with a lodger and had a child by him): The social worker was very kind, *very* understanding. . . . He made me realize that what I had done wasn't so terribly wrong. You see I felt so guilty, not only towards my husband but towards the children. I felt I had let them down. But after I'd been up to see Mr A., I realized that what I'd done wasn't quite so bad.

The emotional support received by these clients appeared to have differing effects. In some instances, the client appeared to feel better about his predicament, although the predicament itself remained unchanged. On other occasions, however, as a result of feeling more confident, the client was able to mobilize his resources and deal more effectively with his problems. Thus, we were told by one client: 'Without her [the social worker] I don't think I could have got over a lot of things that worried me at the time, although she didn't do anything. She just gave me confidence and was always there.' Support can also have instrumental effects when the client feels deeply indebted to the worker for all he has done and, as a means of repaying him, is strongly motivated to change his ways. An apt illustration of this process is provided by Mrs Watt, who, prior to coming to the agency, was unable to plan effectively. Now, however, as a result of her contact, things have changed.

Now when I come out of the FWA after seeing the welfare lady, I plan things and I *do* it. If I promised the psychiatrist [whom she had seen earlier several times and disliked] that I would do something, I would just forget about it. But not with Mrs B. If I say that I'm going to do something, I really do it! [Significantly, she adds] I suppose I do it in order to prove to her that I can because she's been so good to me.

Finally, emotional support sometimes fosters beneficient processes of another sort. As a result of talking with their workers, several clients began discussing their difficulties more openly with family and friends, and this in turn had salutary effects. As a result of their intervention, these workers were indirectly responsible for 'opening-up' the therapeutic possibilities of the clients' own networks.

It is important to note that emotional support cannot be furnished by a worker, or so our data strongly suggest, unless he is perceived in a certain way—specifically, as someone who is interested in the client, as someone who is concerned and really cares (which can be gleaned from our earlier discussion of dissatisfied clients). Mrs Stanton's comments are typical:

She was concerned. And she showed it . . . I mean you get a letter from someone and it says, 'I'm concerned', but when you get there, they've got an entirely different attitude. But there wasn't nothing like this. She was concerned and interested and wanted to help to the best of her ability. And she done that.

What led clients to infer that their workers were concerned? The question is germane since there are no 'natural' or inevitable processes by which the concern of caseworkers (or others) becomes manifest, as witness the dissatisfied clients earlier discussed who failed to detect the concern (or what we can assume was the concern) of their workers. An activistic approach on the part of the worker was repeatedly taken as a sign that he really cared:

The social worker was always taking little notes and she used to say to me, 'Well, go home and think about it and if it's no better the next day, just come and see me and tell me how things are getting on. If it's too bad, we'll solve something, we'll sort something out for you.' *Which I thought meant she must be interested in me—otherwise she would have just listened.* If she wasn't interested, she wouldn't have advised me to do things or offered to come around and see my parents. (Miss Bell)

This general theme is expressed by many clients: workers who wish to help you, expend energy on you in some way. As clients see it, listening does not involve the expenditure of energy.

Enlightenment   Some respondents emerged with a clearer, fuller or in other ways more adequate perception of the troubled situation they were in. Mr West, for example, did not learn anything new about his difficulties from the worker, but he came 'to know his own mind better' as a result of airing his problems. He came to see the issues more clearly, and he had been unable to do this on his own. As he put it: 'When you have a think and ponder all by yourself, you still don't know what you are thinking after you finish.'

In contrast to Mr West, other clients told us they received *new* information from the worker—material which in some way increased their understanding of their situation. On occasion, this information comprised 'facts' about the outside world. One wife learned, for example, that those associating with homosexuals, as did her husband, do not necessarily themselves have tendencies in this direction. Another wife, worried that her ex-husband might gain legal control over her children, was informed that her fears were baseless. Sometimes the information received, instead of stemming from the worker's specialized knowledge, comprised accounts of what was going on in the lives of other people, especially troubled people. Clients were on occasion concerned that they were alone in suffering particular difficulties. They were greatly relieved to learn that 'others were in the same boat', as, for example, Mrs Clifford, who learned that 'it wasn't unusual for marriages to go like hers'. In instances such as these, workers were reshaping the imagery which clients had of other people's lives and in doing this were easing their tensions.

The information received by clients was by no means

confined to 'outside matters'. Sometimes it centred specifically on the client or others involved in the difficulty or some aspect of their relationship. Unfortunately, details are largely lacking concerning the exact ways in which these clients were enlightened, as many expressed themselves in summary form, without elaboration, and their answers were left unprobed, e.g., 'Talking with her showed me things I didn't know about myself.' In view of the failure of the insight-producing procedures, earlier described, to achieve their desired effects, one naturally wonders what clients such as these 'learned about themselves'. One wonders specifically if they came to perceive how they were contributing to their difficulties and if so, the level of insight attained. If it should turn out that any clients were enlightened in this fashion, the finding would be of considerable interest. For it would suggest that insight therapy with working class people might be feasible under certain conditions and the finding might, moreover, identify the particular conditions.

Returning to our data, we are able to spell out at least one way in which clients gained a better understanding of their relationships. On some occasions, they came to have a better appreciation of why the other party (or parties) to the conflict were acting as they were. As workers were sometimes in contact with both 'combatants' (typically marital partners), they were in a position to act as go-betweens, to report facts about one to the other (and occasionally offer interpretations). This process is clearly illustrated in the following description of one worker's principal treatment approach:

> The social worker sort of pointed out things to my husband which he should see and understand in me, and she did the same to me about my husband. For example, she said to me, 'Your husband is also having a hard time. He has had to put up with your mother for quite a long time. He's had your mother in the home and that in itself is quite a difficulty. A man can't possibly feel at home when there's someone watching every move he makes and word he speaks.' You see, my husband is a bit self-conscious anyway —he's inclined to feel a bit inferior and it doesn't help if someone stares at him. He was tense all the time and Miss C. said that it had to come out somewhere in the end. (Mrs Clifford)

7—TCS

One suspects that worker activities of this type play a very significant role in bringing warring spouses together.[4] Persons who are mutually at odds are apt to cut each other off, intentionally or otherwise, from the very information that might lead to a healing of their differences. That is, given the antagonism that exists, it is unlikely that either spouse will provide the other with an accurate picture of his thoughts and feelings (whether out of fear of being hurt or because each assumes the other knows how he feels or some other reason). Fortunately, however, someone who is in contact with both parties (whether a professional worker or a mutual friend) is in a position to undertake this vital service.

Guidance   Finally, evidence suggests that the clients discussed in this chapter welcomed the idea of receiving suggestions, advice and recommendations from the worker.[5] Even though they might not always find the workers' views acceptable, they were none the less anxious to learn exactly what workers felt they should do about their difficulties. A review of our material indicates, moreover, that guidance was offered on a wide range of topics, from which newspaper to buy in order to find job vacancies to the advisability of living with in-laws. Regarding the latter, Mrs Clifford was warned, allegedly, that her mother posed a threat to her marriage and 'would have to go'.

> The social worker said, 'It's unheard of really to have your mother here. I quite understand that you love your mother and that you don't want to push her out on the street, but seriously it's wrong.' . . . She told me it would never work out while my mother was living on the floor with us and I better have a talk with her. . . . She said, 'You've got to be cruel to be kind.'

Clients were especially gratified if the advice received was compatible with that coming from other quarters. (The other side of this coin was noted earlier: clients were disoriented when exposed to conflicting directives from their informal network.) Mrs Stanton, for example, looked upon herself as 'very fortunate', because her various professional consultants (an FWA worker, a solicitor, doctor and housemaster) all agreed on the course she should follow. In the case of Mr Lewisham, both his brother and the worker apparently agreed that the client was overly submissive at home. The fact that their views dovetailed impressed Mr Lewisham, who said of the worker: 'I shall not forget what she said. Because several things she said is the same as John, the brother, would say: "Don't be so foolish. Go out more. Let the woman do the job in the home." ' As a matter of fact, one client initially went to the FWA in order to validate his friend's advice: 'I went to find out whether what David said was right. If they came out more or less the same way as him, then I'd know I was more or less hitting the truth.' (Mr Brown)

Processes uninstigated by the worker

Up to now, our attention has largely centred on satisfaction-producing processes that were expressly set in motion by the worker himself. That is, we can assume that workers explicitly made use of certain treatment procedures, anticipating that these might lead to the results which were in fact later attained. However, it would be a mistake to assume that only processes of this type affect treatment outcomes. Nevitt Sanford, for example, remarks, 'Those who operate an agency for change [e.g., a school, mental hospital or family agency] usually have some kind of theory governing what they do. They bring to bear certain influences which, according to some theory, will change the person in some desired way. But other influences may enter the picture, independently of the therapist or not intended by him and they may have an important bearing on what happens.'[6] Expressing the same thought, Elizabeth Herzog observes that, 'the secret of the practitioner's successes—or of his failures—may lie in features of his practice that are not part of his explicit theory and of which he himself is not aware'.[7] Several of these 'uninstigated' processes came to light in our material; the cases in which they occurred will now be examined.

Mrs Riley was very pleased with her experiences at the agency, because, as a result of her contact there, her husband 'reformed'; he mistreated her less frequently and was less averse to working. According to Mrs Riley, he changed his ways, because he was afraid of what the agency might do if he didn't:

I think it frit [frightened] him when I went. He was worried about my going, in case I could do anything about it. He thinks a lot of the children and he wouldn't be

parted from them for anything. He thought the welfare
might help me to take the children away. . . . Also I
think he was afraid that they might advise me to leave him
and to make a fight to see if I could get the flat. . . .
[Referring to the future, Mrs Riley remarked] I always
say to my husband, even now, 'if you ever give up work
again or do anything to me, I'll go straight to the welfare
officer!' I always say that.

It is plain that the client used the agency to keep her husband
in line. Moreover, because she was successful in her endeavours,
she considered her visits to the FWA worthwhile. In view of
Mrs Riley's 'success', one inevitably wonders if the dissatisfied
clients earlier described attempted to use the agency in a similar
way, and if so, why they (in contrast to Mrs Riley) were not
more successful. In more general terms, it would become
pertinent to explore the following kinds of questions: How do
clients describe an agency's activities to those who are intimately
involved in their difficulties, like husbands and children?
To what extent do they intentionally misrepresent the agency
in an effort to manipulate the other person?[8] To what extent
are their efforts successful? Processes of this type are in need of
study since they may significantly affect client satisfaction (or
dissatisfaction).

Mrs Norton, a young wife in her late teens, told us that she
was shut up all day with her baby in a one-room flat and that
her husband paid little attention to her. If she complained, her
husband refused to listen—he either ignored her, walked out or
told her to 'shut up'. Both husband and wife met with the
worker for two sessions; at the end of this time, Mrs Norton felt
that matters had greatly improved and so, too, allegedly, did
the worker. However, as one reflects on the client's comments,
one senses that the factors responsible for the 'cure' were more
a by-product of the situation than of the worker's design. Specifically, Mrs Norton profited greatly from the fact that the meetings at the FWA enabled her to bring her grievances to the
attention of her husband, something that had previously been
denied her. 'I felt much better down there at the FWA, because
I got a say. If I try to talk to him at home, he always tells me to
shut up. But down there, I got quite a bit off my chest, about
having no money and that.' One might infer that Mr Norton

for once felt obliged to listen to his wife; that is, he probably felt it would not be fitting, in the presence of the worker, to tell her to 'shut up'. But, in addition, Mrs Norton learned things about her husband that had been worrying her. She was concerned that he might be running around with other women. Up to now, she had been unable to get a 'straight' answer from him, but the presence of the worker apparently produced a different result:

> My husband used to tell the gentleman [FWA worker] straight out that he'd never been with a girl. And I knew then that he never had. I believed him because he told that fellow. If he said that to my mum, I took it that he'd be joking, because he's always joking with her. But down there, he come out more plainly—no smiles, no giggles. I took it as the truth then.

Perhaps Mr Norton had been looking for just such an opportunity—that is, an excuse that would enable him to 'level' with his wife. Or perhaps because he felt more kindly disposed towards her as a result of treatment, he wanted *her* to feel better, too, and so put an end to her worries. Yet, it is also possible that he was acting primarily with the worker, not his wife, in mind and thus felt constrained to be truthful. If this were so, we might in a sense look upon his wife as an 'eavesdropper', and, significantly, one whose marriage improved as a result of 'overhearing' remarks of her husband addressed to another person. In short, contingencies of the situation, rather than the specifics of the worker's treatment approach, may have produced the good results achieved.

Let us turn to one final instance in which the client's satisfaction seemingly derived in part from factors uninstigated by the worker. Sociologists have observed that the interaction between persons is sometimes affected by the participants' 'latent identities', that is, by characteristics and statuses that are not supposed, or believed, to play a role in the interaction, but which nevertheless do.[9] For example, the interaction between teachers and students may be affected not only by their 'manifest identities' (being teachers and students) but also by their being men or women, married or single, Negro or white and so forth. A well known example from the mental health field is provided by the Hollingshead-Redlich study in New

Haven. It was found that the type of treatment given to mentally ill persons was determined not only by the specific diagnosis that was made, but also by the patient's social class position.[10]

Social class was relevant in our material also but in a different way. To begin with, the 'superior' social class background of the worker was immediately noticed and typically commented upon by many of the 61 persons we interviewed. Clients frequently made reference to the 'lovely speech' of the worker, to his being 'well spoken' and so forth. However, what is significant from our point of view is that several clients seemingly received a marked psychological lift from the social class differential. The case of Mr Lewisham, a sixty-year-old lorry driver, provides an illustration of this process. In listening to his reverential descriptions of the worker, one has the impression of a nineteenth-century servant talking of the gentry. His interview is replete with comments of this kind: 'When you speak to someone that can speak nicely, it makes a lot of difference', 'She had such a lovely way of speaking', 'An educated person can point things out to you that are really enlightening.' Mr Lewisham describes below how he felt after the first meeting:

> Honestly, I walked out a different person. I must admit I went to a psychiatrist before, it's nothing to be ashamed of, because even the biggest of the big, the greatest, have to go before them, don't they? And sitting and talking to that person [the social worker] was just like being with a psychiatrist. You come out of there feeling on top of the world. Because she was very, very nice.

It would appear, from this and other remarks, that this client was buoyed up not merely by the intentional acts and words of the worker, but in addition by the status differential. One might wonder how frequently instances of this sort occur. We do not know the answer, although one would strongly suspect that they are rarer in the U.S. than in Britain.

A comparison of worker-client interactional patterns

It is apparent that the interactional patterns described in this chapter differed from those earlier considered. An attempt to systematize these differences may be helpful at this point. In the following, we shall compare cases involving satisfied and dissatisfied clients in terms of the main categories used in this chapter: relief from unburdening; emotional support; guidance; and enlightenment. It should be clearly understood at the start that our comparisons must necessarily be crude and impressionistic. We do not have at hand detailed analyses of the workers' activities, of the kind for example, that have been undertaken by other investigators.[11]

With these limitations in mind, let us turn to the first two categories. It would appear that satisfied clients as a rule obtained more relief through unburdening and received also more emotional support. Many of the satisfied clients spontaneously commented on the relief and support they had obtained; conversely, this was rarely mentioned by their dissatisfied counterparts, and when it was, seemed to figure less prominently. This does not necessarily mean that the workers who treated dissatisfied clients actually *offered* less emotional support, although it very well may. It is possible that these workers were trying to be as supportive as the others, but that the various misunderstandings that emerged rendered their efforts sterile. As we have tried to show earlier, only workers who are perceived as caring, as being concerned, are in a position to make their supportive efforts felt. What we have just said enables us to add another dimension to our earlier analysis of dissatisfied clients. We suggested then that cognitive differences between worker and client, in leading to a series of misunderstandings, generated anger, resentment and resignation in the client. But in addition, these differences probably nullified, at least partly, whatever support these workers tried to offer. Clients who felt resentful, for example, probably received little solace from the worker's sympathy or 'understanding' attitude.

It seems relatively clear that the satisfied clients, compared to their counterparts, received more guidance. They received suggestions, recommendations, advice and the worker was active on their behalf.

Finally, the satisfied clients received more enlightenment. Their workers made use of a wide range of 'reflective' procedures, and these tended to be successful in enhancing the client's understanding of his situation. Conversely, the reflective processes invoked by the other workers tended to be more narrowly focused. They were designed to convey to the client how he himself was contributing to his difficulty, and, as we have seen, they were unsuccessful. While the two sets of workers tried to engender different types of understanding, we are uncertain as to which set spent more time in this activity. We would surmise, however, that those treating dissatisfied clients were more active in this respect, if only because they spent less time offering guidance and possibly support as well.

At this point we might well consider the following question: why were these particular clients as satisfied as they were? The question is to the point: we earlier suggested that working-class people will tend to have a unicausal-moralistic-suppressive approach to problem solving. This, in turn, demands responses of a certain type from the worker. Ideally, from the client's perspective, the worker should find the other partner (the husband or child) at fault and go on to suggest ways in which their transgressions might be suppressed or better yet help in their suppression. But workers of the satisfied clients did not act in this fashion; or, if they did, certainly not in such a bald and single-tracked manner. How then can one account for the clients' satisfaction? Two general kinds of answers can be suggested. First, the clients' problem-solving conceptions may have departed in varying degrees from the model previously outlined. Compared to the dissatisfied clients, they may have entered treatment with expectations that were closer to persons of middle-class background. But, at the same time, it is important to note that the activity of these workers was not wholly inconsistent with a unicausal-moralistic-suppressive approach. For example, they offered a good deal of guidance—something which working-class people, it seems, both expect and want. In a more general sense, they participated actively in the treatment situation, a good deal more actively than their counterparts.

In conclusion, the picture we have been able to provide of dissatisfied clients is in some ways more revealing. Perhaps this is a result of differences in salience. The dissatisfied clients had little difficulty in pinpointing and elaborating upon the reasons why they were so disappointed and annoyed. Satisfied clients, on the other hand, seemed to have somewhat more trouble in this connection (although this was not always the case). Interestingly enough, the authors of another study report similar findings. They observe that 'a large proportion of people who visited psychiatrists [and benefited] could give no indication of a specific way in which therapy had helped them.'[12] All of this argues for additional and more intensive studies of satisfied clients. Hopefully, these will enhance our understanding of the therapeutic processes involved.

Clients seeking help with material problems

7

The reluctance to seek material help

About a decade ago, Helen Perlman wrote, 'There was a time when, to ask for financial help, the individual had all but to prove himself a victim of some catastrophe or to admit to moral bankruptcy....' She adds that 'within relatively few years, community attitudes about seeking personal help have undergone tremendous change'.[1] Perhaps this is so regarding those who have psychological or interpersonal difficulties. But as far as financial difficulties are concerned, the resistance of the persons we interviewed towards receiving help of this kind was striking. Traditional attitudes seem still to be very much with us, at least within England and the United States.[2] Factual support for this belief is not hard to come by. For example, in a survey of over 2,000 mothers who were receiving public assistance in New York City, 56 per cent agreed that 'getting money from the Welfare makes a person feel ashamed' and 58 per cent were 'bothered by being on Welfare'.[3] In a smaller study of seventeen native-born applicants in the San Francisco Bay area, it was found that 'the respondents were overwhelmingly reluctant to apply for help, and almost all expressed feelings of inadequacy or embarrassment'.[4] Typical of their attitudes were comments such as these: 'I thought about it for a long time, and cried for days before I picked up the phone to call the Community Chest . . . I was just too proud.' Or, 'I didn't like it, but I had no choice . . . I was the only one in my family who ever had to ask for anything.'[5] If attitudes like these are characteristic of those who actually solicit help, one can imagine the resistance of those who feel they need it but do not apply.

In this chapter we shall return to the pre-treatment phase of the clients' lives and examine the resistances they experienced towards receiving material help. Certain aspects of the pre-treatment stage, it will be recalled, have already been examined. We have seen, for example, that inadequacies in the clients' informal network generated a readiness to seek help; and that the clients' movement towards the FWA was further advanced by referral agents in one way or another. Chronologically, the present discussion belongs with these earlier influences. However, there are certain advantages in having postponed it until now. Unless one understands and constantly keeps in mind the help-seeking attitudes which these clients brought into the treatment situation, it is impossible to make sense of their later reactions to treatment. Accordingly, rather than risk the possibility of the reader forgetting, we have put our discussion off until this point.

The decision to solicit material help from the FWA was not reached rapidly; typically, only after considerable struggle, and even then it was often postponed. As a matter of fact, several persons nearly turned back after reaching the doorstep of the FWA. Mr Peel vividly recalls how he felt before crossing the threshold: 'It was a terrible feeling going. . . . When you knock on the door and they say, come in, you really get pitched up. You feel like going out again.' Mrs Canning related her feelings as follows:

> I said to my daughter that I'm almost in two minds
> whether to go or not. Well, she said, you try them, mum,
> and see what happens. But I had butterflies in my tummy
> all the time I was going there and sitting in the waiting
> room for the lady to come there.

Why were these clients so resistant? After all, the FWA exists in order to help troubled people, its personnel are trained, information is treated confidentially and so forth. An observer unfamiliar with the situation might assume that those in need of help would flock to agencies like the FWA without the slightest hesitation. Why then was this not the case? Our interview material suggests that three different factors were involved. These are actually interwoven, but it is useful to separate them for purposes of analysis.

First, many viewed their financial dependency as a disgraceful admission that they could no longer fend for themselves. Before coming to the agency, they had taken pride in the fact that they had 'always earned their own money', that 'they had never had to ask before'. Now they felt that they were in the degrading position of having to throw themselves on the mercy of others. Over and over again, they talked about the humiliation of being in such a position. To many, it was tantamount to begging:

> I felt belittled by going there. It's just like me going up to you and saying, 'Can you give me some money for this [holds out an ashtray]?' Who am I to you that you should turn around and help me? (Mrs Hunter)

> We never really needed money before I fell out of work. I've always worked for it before and never had anything for nothing. But to go for money, to ask them to help you out, seems a right predicament to get into. That was the worst feeling of it. . . . It's like going out in the middle of the road and singing and expecting someone to give you money. (Mr Peel)

The clients' shame was compounded by the fact that they were going (or considering going) to a social agency for help, instead of to a more 'neutral' source such as friends or relatives. By coping in this manner, they would become 'clients'. That is, in their view, they would become similar to others who sought material assistance, at least in the eyes of many. How were 'clients' visualized by the persons we interviewed? We did not explicitly explore this topic, but our data suggest that clients are apt to be viewed as comprised of two types. First, there are those who are desperately hard up and who, for the most part, are to be pitied. A typical description is provided by Mr George:

> I think the welfare place is more or less a place for anybody with a family that's hard up, in great need, or desperate. Say perhaps someone who is going to be put into the street, with kiddies or something like that.

Secondly, 'clients' consist of 'moral reprobates'—people who are objectionable either because of their social characteristics, their habits, or ways of behaving. Those who are 'drunk all the time' or 'abandon their children' were among the examples cited. Without any question, however, the most frequently cited example consisted of 'cadgers'—people who do not deserve help but who try to bluff the worker into believing they do. A typical description is provided by Mrs Wilson:

> You see them up at the NAB all the time putting on an act, giving them the old hard luck story. They go up there, white women going with coloured men, things like that—they couldn't care less . . . and they collect and quietly they're laughing away. Then they go there the following week.[6]

Given this imagery of clients, as persons to be viewed either with pity or contempt, it is small wonder that our respondents did not want to become part of this group. Clients, such as Mrs Denton, felt they 'were lowering themselves by going to places like the FWA'. Some, understandably, were anxious that others should not learn of their new status. Mrs Blore, for one, did not want her family to know, adding 'Once you go to places like that, you are properly down, you've gone under. That is what people think.' Mr and Mrs Sendall likewise hid the facts from their family:

> We did not tell them because the whole idea of the FWA means that you are in trouble. We would not have wanted the family to find out, because we did not want that much disgrace. I mean there's no crime in being in debt or going to the FWA. But because being in debt was our fault, I suppose, we did live in fear of people finding out.

Mrs Adam vividly recalls how she felt when she was chatting with friends:

> It's very degrading getting help. You feel that everyone is against you and won't talk to you, because you're nothing. I would be standing and having a chat with friends and as they walked away, I would say to myself, well, you're down and everyone is against you. Afterwards, of course, you realize that they know nothing about your affairs, but at the time you feel very low. It's a terrible feeling.

Aside from the shame of economic dependency and the ignominy of becoming a client, there was still another reason why our respondents dreaded the prospect of becoming a client. They anticipated that their transactions with the worker would be painful, for two somewhat distinct reasons. First, many assumed that the worker would react in a moralistic, punitive manner. Mrs Hastings, for one, expected to encounter 'strict women who were very fussy'. She felt the worker would look down on her and treat her as 'some kind of peasant'. Mr and Mrs Sendall expected a 'telling off'. Mrs Sendall added: 'I thought that they would turn around and say that in our position we should know better and should not have got into this mess.' Mr Forest assumed the worker would be an 'old fogey type and rather Victorian'. In revealing that he suffered from chronic bronchitis, she would probably retort: 'get a light job—you can breathe!' With great consistency, the social worker was viewed as someone who would undoubtedly be 'strict', 'stern', and 'abrupt'. Secondly, clients expected to be closely questioned about their economic circumstances and in some instances to have their homes inspected. Not infrequently, this was viewed as a necessary evil; that is, if workers are to dispense help, they understandably must ferret out the most needy or deserving.[7] On some occasions, however, it was feared that they might become over-zealous, even punitive, in their efforts and that something similar to an inquisition would take place. Mr Forest was among those who had expectations of this type:

> Well, I thought, honest to the Gospel, that she would check on every part of my life—the ins and outs of everything. I thought they'd pry—do I drink, do I smoke, how many women have I divorced. . . . I imagined people coming to my address, saying, Does he live here? Is the light off? Try the switches! . . . That was one of the things that stalled me off. I thought to myself, I can't go through all that— everyone's entitled to a bit of privacy.

One inevitably wonders where clients obtained these views about social workers' attitudes and methods of work. To begin with, perhaps they were attributing their own views to the workers. Since clients tended to be disdainful of those who are economically dependent, especially if they go to social agencies, they may have assumed that others, including their workers, would have similar viewpoints. This might explain in part why they expected the worker to be so punitive and in some instances prying. Specifically, if those who go to social agencies are 'moral reprobates', then it would be 'natural' for the worker to act in a punitive fashion. Or if they are 'cadgers', it is understandable that workers would be zealous in their investigatory efforts. This general explanation, having to do with the extrapolation of viewpoints, receives support from other studies. It has been suggested that working-class people, compared to those in the middle class, have a less differentiated view of reality, that they tend to generalize their perspective indiscriminately to other people. 'Lower-class persons,' Schatzman and Strauss observe, 'display a relative insensitivity to disparities in perspective. . . . They take for granted that their perceptions represent reality and are shared by all who are present.'[8] Not unlikely, processes of this nature were operating in the situation in hand (as well as in cases earlier considered in which a unicausal-moralistic-suppressive approach to problem solving was attributed to the worker).

No doubt, more specific elements contributed to the clients' imagery as well, one of which came to light in our material. The following persons had had unpleasant experiences at other agencies and anticipated a repetition at the FWA:

> I thought down there [at the FWA] it would be like the Social Security. They are very abrupt there. You are told to go to a certain place and sit there. Then they call your name out, and you talk in front of other people. That's it—then out you go. They don't really want to know about you. (Mr and Mrs Peel)

> I thought the FWA would be like the Social Security. Down there they talk to you as if you were nothing. I don't suppose they mean to, but I suppose they get so fed up with everybody telling them stories. And another thing, at the Social Security you have to keep telling your story to different people. Nothing's worse than telling your story to different people. You feel that you are begging each time. (Mrs Wood)

The influence of previous experiences is further illustrated by Mrs Watt: 'I thought there'd be about four women sitting in a room and you'd sit in front of them, like a court. After telling them your problem, I thought they'd send you out of the room and then they'd all discuss it. Then they'd call you back in and maybe say, "Well, we will see you such and such a time." ' When asked where she received these impressions, she replied:

> When we was kids we all used to go up to the WVS for clothes. All of us would be trotting along the High Street, but I used to linger at the back because High Street Kensington is a very posh district and that is where we went. Everybody used to look at us—we were all in half rags ... I remember people used to go one by one to the WVS and there was all the old ladies there, dressing you up in all these second-hand clothes.

To sum up, clients seeking material help resisted going to the agency for one or all of the following reasons: Going to the agency was an admission that they could no longer cope and were thus forced to rely on the mercy of others. It meant further that they incurred membership in the client group, with all the added degradation this implied. As if this were not enough, they expected to be treated harshly by the workers. They expected a punitive response and in some instances an invasion of their privacy. This description, we hasten to add, does not apply equally to all clients. Several, for example, came to the agency for less 'humiliating' reasons, e.g., help with budgeting or assistance in getting better housing, and were accordingly less averse to becoming clients. In general, however, most of the clients with whom we talked felt like Mrs Denton who said of social agencies in general, 'It's the last place anybody wants to go unless they are really *desperate*.'[9]

8

Satisfied clients

The striking feature about these clients is that they received what they came for—perhaps not as much as they would have liked, not always in the form they initially wanted, but none the less they did receive material assistance. One can hardly overestimate the important bearing which this had for their feelings of satisfaction. It is no accident that nearly all those who received material assistance were satisfied while nearly all those who failed to receive it were dissatisfied. These clients came to the agency, in spite of strong resistance, because they wanted material help and nothing that happened during treatment altered this fact.[1]

Significant as these economic factors are, two other aspects contributed weightily to the clients' satisfaction. First, clients had expected the process of soliciting material aid to be extremely unpleasant, but it turned out to be much less unpleasant than anticipated. Secondly, in varying degrees they received important non-material benefits from the relationship —unexpected bonuses in the form of relief through unburdening, emotional support, guidance, and enlightenment. These two components can best be discussed collectively and in terms of the clients' perceptions of the worker. Specifically, the clients saw the worker as someone they could talk to, who was interested in them, trusted them, and who lessened their shame.

In the first part of this chapter, we shall illustrate and comment on these particular perceptions. First, however, a word about the use of a 'perceptual' framework at this point, compared to the one earlier used in connection with satisfied clients seeking interpersonal help. In dealing with clients of the latter type, we focused on the *effects* of the worker's activities in so far as these produced satisfaction in clients (relief from unburdening; emotional support; enlightenment; and guidance). Now, however, we shall be dealing with the clients' perceptions. The material emerging from the two frameworks unquestionably overlaps in important ways. For instance, clients who visualized the worker as 'being interested in them' obtained 'emotional support', or so it would certainly seem. Significantly, however, each group entered treatment with a different 'set'. Unlike their counterparts, those seeking material help expected the experience to be painful and humiliating— they expected the very worst. Accordingly, when asked what they thought of their experiences at the FWA or the ways in which they had been helped, they frequently took their expectations into account and compared them to what actually happened. Focusing on their perceptions enables one to bring these discrepancies into view and to reveal the satisfaction-producing effects which they had.

1   To begin with, the worker was typically perceived as 'someone they could talk to', and this often came as quite a surprise:

> Well, I thought that they'd just come, write all the bits on a piece of paper and say to me, 'you pay your creditors so much a week and then you'll be left with so much to live on.' I didn't think they were people you could talk to and feel relieved when you talk to them. . . . I told them a lot of things that I've not told anybody else, about my husband, the beginning of getting married and everything. . . . It was such a relief. (Mrs Brent)

> This talking business really surprised me, because I didn't go there for that. I only went for the electric—to see if they could give me an advance. I didn't know such things went on as this sort of chatting business. No, not at all. Surprised me that did. (Mr Forest)

> Oh, I was so pleased to have someone to talk to. I could tell her anything—more than I could tell my husband. . . . I didn't know there was people like that, that you could go and tell your problems to. . . . I thought the only

welfare there was, was the child clinic—the welfare that comes and visits you in the home. (Mrs Watt)

2   The worker was often seen as someone who was interested in them—someone who really cared and wanted to help. Since perceptions of this type were earlier illustrated in Chapter 6, let us consider instead the source of these perceptions. In other words, what led these clients to conclude that their workers 'really cared'? To begin with, certain clients immediately sensed a friendliness in the air, which was often in marked contrast to other agencies with which they were familiar. Mrs Wood was impressed that the worker at the FWA, unlike the one at the Ministry of Social Security, asked her to sit down and talk with her rather than remain standing. Other clients were impressed with the 'nice' manner in which questions were asked and the fact that the worker did not hurry them. 'It's nice talking to them,' Mr Peel told us. 'You could sit there and talk to them for two or three hours. But at the Social Security, you don't want to know them and they don't want to know you.'

Without question, activity on the part of the worker was the main indicator of interest (which was also true in the case of those seeking interpersonal help). Clients were often aware that efforts were being made on their behalf—for example, that workers were contacting a variety of people (landlords, merchants, gas and electrical employees, local authority officials) in an effort to relieve their financial distress. This is aptly illustrated by one client who exclaimed: 'They *do* things, they don't just talk! They go out and do something for you. You feel as though they're worrying about you.' At least one client overheard the worker in her dealings with creditors and could see for herself that the worker was really trying:

When I told her someone from the electric company had been around to see me, she got straight on the phone and said, 'I told you not to bother Mrs Wood. We're going to pay the bill for her, but it's going to take another couple of weeks.' She really told them off and I thought, she's on my side. . . . I used to think, she's got some go in her. (Mrs Wood)

The very act of providing material assistance (e.g., a grant or loan) was another indicator of interest, in that it strongly suggested to clients that the worker really cared. Mr Peel remarked, 'It's not the thought of her paying a debt for us, it's the thought that they *tried* to help you.' We might add that social workers who are in a position to dispense money are, in some ways, in an enviable position: they have a convenient and ready-made way of demonstrating their interest in the client. A similar thought is voiced by the authors of another study: 'The removal of the income maintenance function from the caseworker may free him to provide more social service but it might also deny him a quick and effective way to win the client's confidence in his intent.'[2]

Several clients had incorrect notions that led them to visualize their workers as extremely interested. Mrs Brent believed that social workers at the FWA are not paid; thus, their activity must be a sign of personal commitment:

> She wanted to help people, because it's voluntary—I mean they don't do it if they don't want to, so they must feel they want to do it. They got a lot of feeling. They'd like to help you even more if it were in their power.

Mrs Globe had incorrect notions concerning the agency's intake policies. She was greatly helped with her marital problems at the FWA, yet believed the agency 'officially' only dealt with cases of material need. After the research interviewer had explained to her that this was not so, Mrs Globe exclaimed with surprise, 'I didn't realize you could go there on this [personal problem]! The welfare lady used to sit and listen, but I didn't know—I thought she was taking a personal interest in me.' These cases can be taken to illustrate a general point: misperceptions may sometimes have beneficial therapeutical results.

3   The worker was viewed as someone who trusted them— someone who was not suspicious of their motives for seeking help and who felt they came with a legitimate grievance. Since these clients were extremely sensitive to any imputation that they might be 'cadgers', the worker's apparent 'faith' in them was of great importance. This is obliquely illustrated by the case of Mr Dale. When we asked him what the worker thought of him, he immediately replied, 'I think she believed I was truthful. I don't think she thought I was telling any lies. I

would hate to think I was wrong about this.' His answer
suggests the salience of the 'honesty' issue and the comfort he
derived from what he believed were the worker's perceptions
of him. One of the reasons that clients believed they were
trusted resulted from a 'non-prying' approach on the part of
the worker. Note, for example, how Mr Peel described his
initial experiences at the agency:

> You go up to the office and tell them your situation, but
> they don't send somebody down to your house who wants
> to see everything. They just ask questions and believe
> you. . . . They seem to know that you're telling the truth.

4 The worker was viewed (or experienced) as someone who
lessened their feelings of shame. Scattered remarks throughout
our interviews suggest some of the ways in which this came
about. As we shall see later, these workers explicitly addressed
themselves to material issues at a very early stage in the treatment process and this presumably lessened the clients' feelings
of shame. It is interesting to note, however, that material
issues can sometimes be broached too early. When Mr Peel
was asked if the worker handled his difficulties in the right
way, he replied:

> When she first asked us a few questions, she didn't ask
> right away the troubles you're in—why were you in debt
> and how did you get into debt and that sort of thing. She
> used a lot of tact. She asked how long we'd been married,
> how many children we've got. She worked around to it
> steady, not blunt like.

The precise manner in which money is given may also
assuage feelings of shame. The case of Mr Dale provides an
example:

> She didn't make me feel embarrassed about accepting the
> money. It wasn't given to me and counted out in one
> pound notes. It was all rolled up in an envelope and put
> in my hand. . . . It was done in such a way that it was
> like a loan. There was an understanding that if at any
> time things went well for me that I would put the money
> [received] back into those little welfare boxes that are
> passed around in different places.

Despite shame-relieving efforts like these, social workers are clearly limited in what they can accomplish. Feelings about accepting 'charity' run deep and are not easily dissipated. For example, Mrs Canning was reassured by the worker that she was not begging. None the less, she remarked, 'I felt better when I had that conversation with the lady, but not as I should have felt. I always had the idea of begging at the back of my mind.' Another client said (Mrs Sendall), 'My husband and I felt we were cadging, but it wasn't the worker who made us feel this way. It's the feeling that anybody would get. It's just a natural feeling that you've been cadging.'

To sum up briefly, these clients received what they came for —material assistance. In addition, their interactions with their workers, relative to receiving help, were a good deal less unpleasant than expected. Moreover, in some instances they received important non-material benefits as well. These three factors account for their satisfaction.

At this point, it may be useful to look at these cases over time. When the cases are viewed longitudinally, something of a progression comes to light, with each case (roughly speaking) moving through similar stages. This kind of regularity, one might note, was seemingly less characteristic of other cases studied. Below, the various stages to which we are referring will be outlined in schematic form.

1   The material needs of the client were given early consideration. Mrs Globe, for example, related that the worker, at the end of the first interview, said: 'Don't worry too much about it —we will give you a certain amount towards this bill.' Mr Dale's worker allegedly said: 'Come and see me again and I'll put your case to some committee to see whether we can help you.' Certainly the promise or possibility of help was important, but the point we wish to make is of another type—namely, that the workers in these instances were giving immediate consideration to the clients' needs as they defined them. There was one instance, in fact, in which a client was told right at the start that there was little possibility of his obtaining material assistance. While disappointed, he was not angered—unlike clients to be considered later whose needs (as perceived by them) were only confronted at a later point, if at all.

2   Once the worker had given consideration to the client's

needs, our evidence suggests that the client, not the worker, made the next 'move'.

> She said, 'If there's anything you want to confide in me, please feel free to do so. . . .' I didn't have to tell her anything I didn't want to. She didn't ask me anything— just about the debts, that's all. She had to know anyway, because it had to be worked out. But as for everything else, that was entirely up to me. (Mrs Brent)

> After the bill for the electric was paid, she said, 'Would you like to see me again for a chat' and I said, 'Yes indeed', because she's evidently been trained for the job and she knows about problems. . . . Then once she said to me, 'Do you think these interviews are doing any good?' and I said, 'Yes, indeed.' We used to chat for an hour, very intimately too, things that I wanted to tell her, that I could only tell her. (Mr Forest)

> It was quite nice to sit and talk with him. . . . We used to sit and I think gradually we got more into my personal life. He used to say, 'If you're worried or troubled, let me know.' (Mrs Globe)

3   The worker's handling of the new material was 'meaningful to the client.

Frequently the problem which the client brought to the agency was broadened or extended in some way. Sometimes this was merely a matter of the client airing his anxieties about his economic difficulties. On other occasions, however, the client branched off into other directions, frequently dwelling on troublesome aspects of his marital or family life. Notably, in all but one instance, the worker's response was 'meaningful' to the client and can readily be subsumed under the categories which we have earlier made use of, i.e., relief through unburdening, support, guidance, and enlightenment (minus 'self-understanding').

The following examples illustrate both the branching out process and the positive effects of the worker's approach. Mrs Wood, who initially came to the agency for help with an electric bill, found she was later talking about 'silly little things that were on her mind'. She adds: 'You sit there and you talk and you might say, "Oh, I'm worried about this and my husband's

inside [in prison]." When you come out, you feel it's not half
so bad.' Mr Forest initially sought help with an electric bill, too,
but after a few interviews he was discussing his personal plight—
after twenty-five years of marriage, his wife had suddenly
deserted him and he was confronted with having to make an
adjustment. Among other things, the worker offered advice
which he felt was 'excellent'—for example, he should try to
immerse himself in his work and see his family and children as
much as he could. Mrs Globe originally came to the agency,
because she was 'frightened that the gas might be turned off'.
At a later period, however, she was describing the unsatisfactory
nature of her marriage and her tentative plans to separate
permanently and perhaps remarry. Aside from offering a
sympathetic ear, the worker raised certain questions about her
plans that she had not earlier considered. These were much
appreciated and led to her pursuing a different course. Perhaps
the best way of revealing the positive effects of the workers'
approach is to examine the one exception. Mrs Mountford
(whose interview is reproduced in Appendix 4) greatly appreciated the material help she had been given, but had one
reservation:

> The only thing is [the worker from the FWA] seemed to
> have an obsession about feelings. Everything that arose,
> or every statement that we made, it was always, 'Well,
> what are your feelings about this?' . . . I couldn't
> understand what this had to do with our case, because I
> didn't think it was helping us in any way.

Before concluding this chapter, an additional feature of these
cases deserves attention, one which we have been unable to
subsume under our earlier discussion. Perhaps half a dozen
clients commented that their feelings of gratitude led them to
prolong their contact with the worker beyond what they felt
was necessary. In this connection, Mrs Paul remarked, 'We
didn't want to accept their help and then cast them aside.'
Or Mrs Mountford: 'We didn't really like to say to him, well
we don't need your help any more, because it seemed as if we'd
used him and weren't grateful. It would seem like we got what
we could and then was going to dispense with him.' She was
additionally reluctant to break off, because the worker was
visiting her rather than her visiting the agency. Presumably

this made it more difficult for her to disengage herself in a tactful manner or so her comments suggest: 'As long as he was willing to come to us, we were willing to see him. We didn't like to tell him that we no longer needed his services.'

Feelings of indebtedness may also lead those who *have broken off* to feel rather guilty about it. Mrs Hastings stopped going to the agency for the following reasons: her pregnancy made it increasingly difficult for her to travel; the worker with whom she had contact was in the process of leaving the FWA; and she felt that she had been greatly helped. She, nonetheless, had qualms about not returning:

> Sometimes it runs through my mind that they helped me out and I shouldn't ignore somebody that's helped me. Just because you've got over your troubles, you don't stop seeing somebody.

It is worth considering these processes in wider perspective. To begin with, it is commonly recognized that feelings of indebtedness on the part of the client may have beneficial treatment effects. For example, a client may be ready to drop out; yet, feelings of obligation may lead him to continue. Or, in order to please the worker, he may adopt new behavioural patterns, as was the case with Mrs Watt who remarked, 'I suppose I do it [plan more effectively now] in order to prove to her that I can because she's been so good to me.' Social workers are, of course, aware of these processes and may sometimes intentionally make use of them. In this connection, Elizabeth Irvine remarks, 'Some of us do give with strings attached, in terms of some implicit bargain that if we do this for them they will do something for us, make some kind of effort.'[3] Despite their potential value, it is well to realize that efforts of this type may simultaneously produce unwanted effects, as for example those noted above. An awareness of what is happening, however, should enable the worker to take appropriate steps.[4]

9

Dissatisfied clients

In contrast to those just discussed, clients who were dissatisfied did not—save in a few instances—obtain the help which they so desperately sought. Unquestionably this was a major source of their dissatisfaction. But, as has been the case with practically all respondents studied thus far, the realization or non-realization of their initial wishes was not the only factor affecting their reactions to treatment. As we have seen, certain other features of the casework situation, which were partially independent, played an important role in shaping their feelings. Particularly in the case of clients now under review, these additional elements tended to generate anger and resentment. In short, if we are to understand the treatment reactions of these particular persons, in anything approaching a complete sense, we must learn something about the so-called 'additional elements' of the casework process and the reasons why they produced the effects which they did.

In the following we shall present in some detail five different case histories illustrating the influences and processes referred to above, which were operative within the group as a whole. These particular cases were selected because these respondents were very 'open' and provided us, relatively speaking, with a more detailed picture of their feelings and reactions. In certain ways, they (as well as respondents not explicitly discussed) bear a strong resemblance to the other set of dissatisfied clients, those who sought help in dealing with someone else. In order to bring out the various similarities as well as dissimilarities, at least the more important ones, we have put these cases in a certain order. Those that are described at the start are intended to reveal processes already depicted; these, we trust, will be familiar and require little comment. The cases subsequently presented are intended to bring out processes that were more characteristic, in the main, of clients seeking material help, specifically dissatisfied ones. These divisions are not hard and fast. There is a good deal of overlapping. None the less, this manner of presenting our material will hopefully enable the reader to make use of what has gone before, before being introduced to a fresh set of considerations.

Before proceeding, a word about the workers treating the clients discussed in this chapter. Most, but not all, made use of an insight-oriented approach and were thus essentially similar to those earlier described.

Case histories

Mrs Hunter is a woman in her middle twenties with three children. She went to the FWA because she was in 'terrible debt', due to her husband's gambling, and 'couldn't stand the strain and worry of the debts' any longer. She was desperately hoping that she might obtain a loan from the FWA. A chance encounter with a stranger (which was described in an earlier chapter) led her to believe she might be successful. The stranger, 'a woman at the laundry', had earlier been to the FWA, and assured the client that she, too, 'was bound' to be helped.

Mrs Hunter describes below what happened at the FWA:

> I got very upset and poured out lots of feeling—I can tell you I poured out my life to them, my debts, my worry, what was going on at the time. . . . All they seemed interested to me was that they just wanted to know my personal life, what we were like, what we argued over and that was all. If you want my honest opinion, as far as I was concerned, all they wanted to know about was what was going on in *my* life and that was all. It was just like the woman up the road wants to know what's the matter with Mrs Jones, so she comes down and asks me about it. . . . I can't explain it, I felt like it just fell on deaf ears. Do you understand what I mean? I felt like it from the start, after the first interview. I felt, well it's just no good.

Mrs Hunter mentioned that she did not explicitly tell the worker (referring to one worker in particular) that she hoped to obtain material assistance. When asked why, she explained:

> Look, let's face it. If I'm going to sit here and tell you all my money worries and explain to you that if we got out of debt that we would be happy ever after and you had that money in front of you, you would know damn well that's what I was after, wouldn't you? Let's face it. Why didn't I say it outright? I mean that man's got intelligence. That's what he's there for. He's there to see between the lines, apart from what I'm telling him.

Mrs Hunter apparently assumed that the worker would see things as she did. That is, once he appreciated the desperate nature of her plight, he would agree that material help of some kind was the only possible answer to her difficulties. That being the case, there was little need for her to articulate her wishes. Feelings of shame, however, also contributed to her reticence: 'I felt belittled by having to go there—I was begging as far as I was concerned. . . . I thought if they were there to help me, *they* would suggest it.'

The respondent offered several reasons to explain why the workers focused on her personal life. As already noted, the workers were considered 'nosey'—which, in terms of our earlier scheme, is another way of saying that they were not really interested in her. Then again, perhaps the FWA, as a matter of policy, did not deal with difficulties such as she had. Note, for example, Mrs Hunter's response when asked if she felt the workers handled her difficulties in the right way:

> To be honest with you, I can't put an answer to that question. I might have been the wrong type of case to go there. . . . I mean they sort out your marriage problems and things like that but maybe they don't want to deal with people who just have debt and worry because that really was my main problem. . . . You might think I was damn cheeky even thinking they would pay my debts and things like that. But I was told that is what they were there for and they would help me and so I tried and I got nowhere and I didn't bother to go any more.

The processes revealed in the following case closely parallel those just described. Mrs Hall left her husband nearly twenty years ago and for many years has lived with her daughter, an only child, now in her thirties. The client came to the agency hoping for financial help. She was currently unable to find work and felt very guilty that her daughter had to contribute so much of her income to maintaining the household. In her opinion, financial assistance of some sort would help to take the load from her daughter's shoulders. When asked about the likelihood of obtaining help, she responded, 'Well, I know people *have* been helped. You read things in the newspapers and you hear of people being helped. I mean I don't expect people to help anyone, but if other people are getting it and I was in difficulties—well, I just wondered.'

Mrs Hall was asked what she talked about when she first went to the FWA:

Well, he just let me ramble on. . . . But after the first visit, it seemed a bit pointless. It seemed as if he was there just for the purpose of hearing my worries and troubles. He *didn't* say, 'Well, after I've heard all the circumstances, I will help you in any way you need.' He didn't say that, not in so many words—at least, he didn't give me the impression that he would help in that way. I just talked to him and he said, 'Would it be any help if I saw your daughter?' Well, my daughter didn't want anything. *I* was the one who needed the help, but he seemed to speak as though my daughter and myself weren't getting on too well together. But that wasn't the problem. He sort of misunderstood in a way. There was nothing he could do to make the two of us happier—we are close and fond of each other and we do study each other's feelings. The only thing—you might call it the fly in the ointment—was the lack of security, that nagging worry. . . . (*What did the worker think should be done about this?*) Well, he couldn't make any suggestions. You see the only thing that could help us was money. I know that doesn't sound very nice, but it was the *only thing* that could help us. (*Were you able to say this to him?*) No, no, I wasn't that put at ease. . . . But he understood that this was what I wanted—I went around it without mentioning the word if you know what I mean. Oh, yes, he knew the worry.

Why didn't the worker address himself to financial issues? Mrs Hall put forward a number of reasons. Because he was so young and inexperienced, the worker was unable to appreciate the viewpoint of an older person, specifically, how distressed someone like herself might be in having to impose such burdens on a daughter. But, in addition, Mrs Hall wondered, and was still wondering when we interviewed her, if she might not have inadvertently solicited help from the wrong place:

> Well, I thought that I'd gone to the wrong department for help. They don't deal with financial worries at the family welfare, do they? It's more for incompatibility, isn't it? . . . I think that if a husband drank or was work-shy or something like that, I think this young man would have done an awful lot to help the husband and wife to understand each other. But in my case, it wasn't a case of my daughter and myself not understanding each other— we understand each other very well. . . . There's nothing anyone can put right except help. Security. Just security.

Mr and Mrs Adam are a middle aged couple with five children. For many years now, Mr Adam has operated a stall in the market place during spring and summer, selling merchandise. Because of illness and unemployment during the winter, Mr Adam lacked the money to buy stock for the following spring when it would be time again to open the stall. The couple, after borrowing from members of the family, went to the (then) NAB who, in turn, referred them to the FWA.

Below we have reproduced verbatim an exchange that took place during the very early part of the interview. It pointedly reveals the puzzlement and disorientation experienced by the clients, due to the worker's shifting the focus of attention. The exchange is of interest, because the respondent (Mrs Adam) spontaneously launched into topics that were usually initiated by the research interviewer himself and at a much later point. The client's early raising of these issues suggests their salience.

Interviewer Did you have any idea how the Family Welfare go about helping people?

Client	No.
Interviewer	I mean did you suddenly expect them to turn up with a cheque book?
Client	Well, I didn't really know what to expect. As I say we knew nothing about it until this lady came.
Interviewer	She came to see you?
Client	Well, my husband went over to the office, and they said they would send someone to interview me. Well, for a while, I thought that the lady thought that the family was breaking up over it, questions like what she asked, and I tried to explain that it was nothing like that.
Interviewer	What sort of questions did she ask?
Client	Well, what was our marriage like, were we happy together, were the children contented and things like that. It had nothing to do with what we wanted. It was financial help not any other help. We were trying to explain to her, but she didn't understand, well I don't think she understood about the stall and the stock money. Well, eventually I think she got the hang of it like.
Interviewer	Now that was the first time she came?
Client	Yes, but every other time she came, she was still talking about the stock money and what we meant by it. She didn't understand what we were talking about really.
Interviewer	And she thought it was all to do with your marriage?
Client	Well, that's what my opinion is, anyway. . . . Well, it upset me and I said to my husband, 'Did you say our marriage was breaking up or something?', and he said 'No, why?' And I told him about the questions the lady had asked and he said she had asked him about the same questions too, and he found it funny too. Up until then we hadn't discussed what the lady had asked him and what she had asked me and when we talked about it, we found

	that she had asked the same questions to us and we had both really gave the same answers. (*Tape inaudible*)
Interviewer	So she really got hold of the wrong end of the stick?
Client	I think so.
Interviewer	Was she a young person or an old person?
Client	No, she was young. At first I thought she was a psychiatrist or something like that.
Interviewer	Did you? What made you think that?
Client	Well, the questions she asked, and I thought to myself, it's the questions she's asking—they have nothing whatsoever to do with financial help, nothing at all.
Interviewer	What was it like, having her come here and ask this sort of question?
Client	Well, it makes you feel, well very humble, very degraded, you know—and as I say when you are not used to going to these places, well it takes a lot out of you to pick up courage to go.
Interviewer	Did it upset you very much?
Client	Yes, it did upset me, and my husband was very upset. It takes a lot to go to one of these places. You feel very beholden to someone. I don't know if you should feel like that, but we felt it at the time.

Mrs Adam believed the worker was questioning her about her marriage, because she (the worker) was unable to grasp the true nature of her difficulties. This theme was amplified at a later point when Mrs Adam said:

I think that if you are going to have someone interview you and you need help like that, they should send someone who has a family and has gone through this and knows much more about it. Now this lady, I suppose, has been to college and had a good upbringing and was never short of money. . . . But they don't know what it is to be short of money. . . . I think they should go through a course of being in a family and see what happens. They just don't understand.

Mrs Adam's efforts to understand the worker's behaviour took another form as well. She felt the worker was checking up on her veracity:

> I knew she had to ask *some* questions—for instance, we might never have been married and she was trying to find out if we really were married. . . . I told myself that she had to find out if we were really genuine. . . . However, if she had gone deeper, I wouldn't have answered the questions. Perhaps I would have got angry then and told my husband about them—but it didn't go that deep.

The belief on the part of clients that they were being cross-examined (when they were in fact not) was shared by many in our group. Clients like Mrs Adam were ashamed that they had to solicit financial aid and felt that they were begging. Moreover, they often feared that, in the eyes of the worker, they would be considered worthless and disreputable. Their later conclusions (or suspicions) to the effect that they were not trusted presumably confirmed their earlier fears. Without some such interpretation, it is difficult to account for the vehemence of one of Mrs Adam's concluding remarks. She told us that she would let her children starve before seeking professional help again. This remark, it should be noted, was made despite having received a £20 grant from the agency.

Another of the client's remarks, drawn from an earlier section of the interview, merits attention. In what struck us as a perceptive comment, the client observed: 'My husband was very upset by the marriage questions and he *looked* so upset that I suppose the lady got the impression that he was on the verge of breaking down or something. . . .' While data are lacking, it is not unlikely that Mr Adam's reactions confirmed the worker's suspicions that the couple's difficulties *were* ultimately marital, not financial. If so, this would comprise a prototype of the kinds of processes that were repeatedly operating in many of the cases surveyed in our study. The worker anticipates that his questions will fall on a sensitive area and provoke the client. When the client is in fact provoked, the worker, unaware of the precise manner in which he is functioning as a catalytic agent, views the client's reactions as supporting his initial hypotheses. One is reminded of the psychiatrist with bad breath who uniformly found indications of 'negative transference' in his clients, as evidenced by their withdrawal.

Mrs Gore is thirty years old, the mother of three children and recently separated from her husband. Before separating, she and her husband had bought furniture on hire purchase, but after the separation, her husband refused to make any payments. Mrs Gore was unable to meet the payments, and the company was threatening to take her to court over the matter. Mrs Gore went to the FWA, via the CAB, hoping for financial help.

Although the client had never heard of the FWA, she had fairly definite thoughts as to what would happen once she got there. First, she expected that someone from the agency would come down to her place in order to 'look around'. Secondly, she expected to be questioned along certain lines: 'I knew they would ask questions. If they're going to give you money, they don't give it to you just like that. I thought they'd ask whether I could go to work, if I had seen my husband about the furniture and things like that.'

Mrs Gore saw two different caseworkers, both of whom were 'very nice'. However, the interviews themselves were a different matter—in her opinion they were highly distasteful and a waste of time:

It's just that the ladies used to ask me the same questions every time I see them: how much do I owe, how much do I pay out, how much do I put in the electric light, how much do I put in the gas. . . . Then they also asked me about the children, about myself, and my husband—how long had I been married, how long was I separated, and things like that. Every time I would see them, they would ask the same old questions over and over again. (*Were you asked what sort of help you wanted?*) Yes, it was discussed. (*And what did they say about this?*) They didn't sort of answer it. Well, every time I mentioned about the furniture, they just sort of went into something else. . . . They just didn't seem interested in me getting into debt and having to go to court.

Mrs Gore answered the workers' questions as best she could, because she felt she had to co-operate if she were to receive any help. She was, none the less, irritated by the personal nature of some of the questions: 'I just thought they were being nosey, wanting to know the ins and outs of everything. . . . I thought, it's nothing to do with them. I didn't go up there because of my marriage, I only went there to see if they could help me out.'

She went on to explain why, in her opinion, the workers were repeatedly going over the same ground and questioning her so closely: 'I thought they were just trying to catch me out, to see whether I was lying or not.' When asked what would happen if the workers *did* catch her out, she replied: 'I just thought they would turn around and say, "Well, we can't help you." ' Mrs Gore mentioned a number of times that the workers' questioning made her 'nervous'. It is easy to understand why: since she felt she was being cross-examined, she was under continuous pressure to be consistent in her responses. One might add that client reactions of this type are hardly conducive to therapy, whether of the insight or supportive variety. Successful therapy presumably demands at least *some* spontaneity from the client. Mrs Gore, however, was constantly 'on guard', lest she inadvertently contradict herself.

Finally we shall describe the case of Mrs Wilson, which in many ways is one of the most revealing in our study. Apart from providing additional support for earlier interpretations, it brings into sharp focus some additional dissatisfaction-producing processes. Mrs Wilson is twenty-three years old and the mother of two children. At the time of the study, her husband was in prison, on a six-month sentence. She went to the FWA (having been referred by the NAB), because she was having difficulty 'making ends meet' and above all wanted help with a large electricity bill.

In order to make sense of Mrs Wilson's reactions to treatment, one must attempt to understand her views about 'entitlement'. Mrs Wilson as well as members of her family (especially her mother and sisters) felt she was entitled to have her electricity bill paid by the FWA, if not entirely, at least in part. In this connection, the client's mother allegedly stated: 'You're entitled to it, you know. You go around and see them.' Among the factors responsible for the client's views concerning 'entitlement' were the following: first, no one in the Wilson family had ever been on national assistance before; this meant to the client that money that she and her family had put into the government had never been withdrawn and was in fact 'owed' her. Secondly, the Wilsons, unlike others who apply for help, were felt to be particularly deserving and for the following reason: 'Nobody in the family had ever been away in prison before—my husband was the first. No man had ever walked out, they've always been together.' Thirdly, Mrs Wilson felt she was seeking help for a serious, not a frivolous, reason: 'I didn't go for clothes for myself or anything silly, like carpets and floors. It was sensible for what I went. It was a needy thing, so why shouldn't I get it?' Although Mrs Wilson felt 'entitled', she recognized that many persons come to the agency —in fact, many more than can be served. In her view, it was the worker's job to sift out the most needy or deserving.

All told, the client had eight interviews at the FWA, with two different workers, and received considerable financial help, forty pounds to be precise. These payments were unquestionably appreciated, but the casework process itself generated considerable resentment. The first worker apparently approached matters on a practical level, at least initially, by suggesting various ways in which the client might economize as well as augment her income. For example, the worker suggested that Mrs Wilson should return some recently acquired furniture that had been bought on hire purchase; that she place her child in a nursery so that she could work; and that she consider taking in a boarder. Each of these suggestions was bitterly resented, because they were interpreted as efforts, on the part of the worker, to get rid of her—to 'slough her off', instead of attending to the requests with which she came. Mrs Wilson was additionally incensed by the worker's seemingly innocent suggestion that it might relieve her isolation (due to her husband's imprisonment) if she took more meals with her relatives. The client assured us that, despite what the worker might think, she was *not* a cadger—she was not one to sponge free meals from those in the family.

Significantly, Mrs Wilson did not express resentment for, according to her, this would jeopardize her chances of getting help. Note, for example, the following exchange:

I couldn't keep letting her see it [her annoyance.] She would have felt, well, we won't give her any help at all and that's it. (*So you thought that if you showed . . .*) Yes, I wouldn't get anything. (*Did you feel she could hold it back in some way?*) Yes, the way she used to say, 'We are only allowed to give a certain amount of money out.' That always made me feel as though she wouldn't give it if she didn't have to, *really have to*.

In order to increase her chances of getting help, Mrs Wilson utilized a number of 'ingratiating' techniques, several on the advice of her mother:

Once when I was going, Mum said to me, 'Take the boy with you, but don't put that coat on him—she'll think you are well off, that you are only there for the extra money.' Mum said, 'Don't get him done up. You're supposed to look rough when you go to those places.' (*Why did your Mum think this was so?*) Because if you look poor, ever so poor, you get it, and Mum was afraid I wouldn't get it. (*Do you think your Mum was right?*) Well, it is right, isn't it? Well, *I* think it's right . . . for the simple reason Mum should know, because she's been out in the world. So I took her advice. I took his coat off and put his old one on. And I got help.

There were several other occasions in which the client was coached by her mother, among them the following: 'Mum said to me once when I was going, "Now don't be saucy, just answer her questions. Don't speak out of turn or you won't get it." '[1]

The second worker apparently spent more time exploring the client's family relationships, particularly her marital relations, and was resented even more than the first:

During the last two interviews, they put me in touch with this young one. She was nice and yet she made you feel low like. She nearly had me in tears the last time I came out, with the things she was saying. All she kept on about was, 'Oh, so your husband isn't home? When will your husband be done?' She said, 'I've got it all written down on a paper in front of me, but you can tell me yourself', and all the time I was speaking about my husband I was getting choked.

The worker's probing into her marital life was resented on a number of grounds. First, it was irrelevant: 'I didn't go there for nothing else but the electricity bill! She didn't have to speak about everything else!' Secondly, it was redundant—the worker (as well as her predecessor) had already collected the information requested, so there was no need to ask for it again. Thirdly, the questions were 'improper':

> *I* wouldn't have asked questions like that. She shouldn't
> have kept harping on it, like 'How do you feel', 'How
> do you manage', 'How does your husband feel', 'How is
> he when you go to see him.' You don't ask questions like
> that, not even if you're a welfare woman. You're not
> entitled to ask people questions like that, are you really?
> Well, I don't think you are. . . .
> It's nothing of their interest what he's like when you go to
> see him anyway.

Mrs Wilson contrasted the worker's behaviour with that of her family:

> Mum wouldn't say to me, 'What's it like when you go and
> see him?' She wouldn't say anything like that. In fact, none
> of the family really talk about it. They just say: 'Have you
> heard from him?' 'How is he?' Or if he is coming up on
> hostel, 'Did he get past?'—something like that, but not all
> the time keeping on about it.

Finally, the worker's talking about her husband—in addition to being irrelevant, redundant, and 'improper'—was upsetting. As Mrs Wilson put it, 'she was choked'. There are several hints in this and other interviews that clients do not envision psychological discomfort as in any way leading to long-term therapeutic gains. In this connection it is worth noting what two other researchers have to say:

> A patient who does not understand what is expected of
> him is almost certain to encounter difficulties. . . . If,
> despite all odds, the patient is able to make some progress
> and derive a glimmering of insight, the resultant increase
> in anxiety may be interpreted by the patient as an
> indication that he is getting worse. Thus he may terminate
> the treatment—not because of an unwillingness to tolerate

anxiety, but on the basis of the commonsense conclusion
that something that makes him feel worse does in fact
make him worse.[2]

In any event, once Mrs Wilson felt that there was little chance
of obtaining additional help, she saw no reason to continue.
'If she [the worker] wasn't going to give me no more help with
the electricity bill, I didn't have to stand all that personal, you
know, feeling sort of thing. I wasn't going to sit and talk all
about my husband to her!'

Mrs Wilson's caseworker (the second one) was interviewed
by us, and a review of her comments sheds further light on the
misunderstandings that occurred.[3] Both she and her predecessor
were aware of the client's views concerning her 'entitlement',
but each apparently tended to discount them. For example, the
second worker said, with a note of disbelief in her voice, 'Mrs
Wilson seemed to expect that the worker would pay the bill
with *no doubts* at all!' And at another point, 'I can't believe
that she would expect us to pay the bill a *third time*!'

The client's demands of the agency, according to the worker,
derived from feelings of resentment which were connected with
her husband's imprisonment. Mrs Wilson was allegedly angry
both at her husband and at society—at her husband because
of the position he was in and at society for having unjustly
punished him. Her indignation led her to feel that society owed
her something, and the 'something' became, in the course of
time, the electricity bill. The following excerpts, drawn from
different parts of the interview, give a sense of the worker's
thinking:

> This electricity bill was a terrific projection of all her
> resentments against her husband's being taken away and
> going to prison. She couldn't acknowledge any resentment
> at all, except to somebody who refused to pay her electricity
> bill.

> [Her demands of the agency] were symbolic of the fact
> that society owed her something—because society had
> taken her husband away.

> There must, of course, inevitably be a terrific amount of
> resentment against her husband himself, for having got
> himself into that position, but all she could ever say was,

'I'm absolutely devoted to my husband, there's no problem at all, the only problem is that he's gone to prison and he shouldn't be there.' This was the story over and over again.

The worker told us that neither she nor her colleague were able to 'get through' to the client. For example, 'both the previous worker and myself tried to spell out to her what the payment of the electricity bill meant to her, but she grew angry every time you said it to her'. As in the case of Mrs Adam earlier considered, Mrs Wilson's reactions were very likely taken as support for the psychodynamic propositions put forward by the workers.

The five cases just presented contrast sharply with those considered in the preceding chapter. The latter, it will be recalled, perceived the worker as someone they could talk to; someone who was interested in them; someone who trusted them; and someone who lessened their feelings of shame. Viewed longitudinally, these cases went through a kind of progression: the client's material needs were given early consideration; once done, the client—not the worker—made the 'next move'; and finally, the worker's handling of new material was considered 'meaningful'. Few, if any, of these processes were operative in the cases just described.

A comparison of dissatisfaction-producing processes

Before concluding this chapter, let us compare and contrast the two sets of dissatisfied clients that have been considered in this study. Aside from serving as a review, this will enable us to bring out several additional points.

In many ways the cases considered in this chapter (whether actually described or not) bear a strong resemblance to their counterparts—dissatisfied clients in search of interpersonal help. As a rule, both sets of clients had certain views as to how their problems would be handled and each expected these to be shared by the worker. Those seeking interpersonal help expected the worker to base his actions on a unicausal-moralistic-suppressive approach to problem solving; those in search of material assistance took it for granted that the worker would consider material relief the only possible answer to their plight. Indeed, clients of both types were so certain that workers would see things as they did that on many occasions they felt it unnecessary to articulate their views and desires.

Both sets of clients failed to discern that the worker's actions stemmed from a different system of problem solving. Clients seeking interpersonal help, it will be recalled, were puzzled by the worker's lack of active participation, his focusing on them instead of the 'responsible' party, and his probing into the past. The clients discussed in the current chapter primarily mentioned the worker's shifting the focus of attention. They were bewildered and frequently angered by the fact that the worker, rather than trying to 'help' them, dwelt on totally unrelated matters. Many complained that their workers kept returning to the same topics and raised the same questions over and over again. One can reconstruct what, in all likelihood, was happening. Figuratively speaking, worker and client were engaged in a continuous tug of war, with each trying to bring the conversation back to 'essentials'. When the client tried to direct the worker's attention to his material needs (which feelings of shame occasionally prevented him from doing), the worker probably viewed this as a return to the 'presenting' problem. When the worker tried to involve the client in matters considered more 'basic', the client viewed these excursions as irrelevant and when they persisted as being needlessly repetitious.

To compound matters further, clients of both types were never certain that their hopes might not eventually be realized. For example, they were typically encouraged, at the end of each session, to come in for more visits. Or if they failed to keep an appointment, the worker expressed the hope that another would be made in the near future. These expressions of interest and solicitude were understandably taken as signs that help of an 'appropriate' type might ultimately be forthcoming and incidentally explain why certain dissatisfied clients continued for as long as they did. One such 'continuer', in looking back at her experiences, bitterly remarked: 'If they couldn't help me out the first time, they should have said so and that would be that!'

Finally, both sets of clients tried to make sense of the worker's activities and tended to reach similar (though not always identical) conclusions, e.g., the worker was uninterested in them, distrusted them, failed to understand their problems and so forth. These misinterpretations tended to generate anger and resentment and very clearly impeded the worker's efforts to be helpful.

'Impression Management' Let us turn now to several contrasts. To begin with, we suspect that clients seeking material assistance were more concerned than their counterparts with the impressions they were making on the worker and, as a result, expended more energy on what Goffman has called 'impression management'.[4] Their relatively greater emphasis on creating the 'right' impression stems, in our view, from certain basic differences in the situations confronting the two types of clients.

For one thing, those seeking material help felt (or, at least, vaguely realized) that they were in competition with other clients. They recognized that material help is in short supply and that if their quest was to be successful they would have to appear more 'deserving' than others. In this connection, Mrs Wilson, it will be recalled, made a point of concealing her annoyance at the worker and saw to it that her son was not over-dressed. Other clients behaved, or at least hinted that they behaved, in a similar way. By contrast, those seeking interpersonal help were not involved in a competition of this sort. For example, the fact that a worker 'drums some sense' into a husband's head does not prevent her from doing exactly the same thing in dealing with other clients. Since help of this type is *not* in limited supply, these clients presumably felt less need to manipulate their workers, that is, to present themselves in a certain light in order to attain their ends.

Secondly, we strongly suspect that those seeking material assistance were anxious to escape the effects of their own projections. As noted earlier, these clients tended to believe that their workers would be contemptuous of their financial dependency or, worse yet, look upon them as cadgers. Given these perceptions, we would suppose that they did their best to become 'de-classified'—to become viewed as 'different', as persons who did not *really* belong in the client category. Any success they achieved—which essentially involved efforts to appear 'deserving'—would presumably help them to preserve their self-respect, to say nothing of yielding (or hopefully yielding) financial benefits. Those seeking interpersonal help, on the other hand, did not attribute punitive views to the workers and for this reason probably had less need to exercise control over the impressions they were creating.

This emphasis on 'impression management' is perhaps fairly general among clients in need of material help. In this connection, one observer notes: '... even when one is giving help free, either monetary assistance or some service such as therapeutic casework or medical examination, one should expect at least a partially calculative orientation. Many clients are likely to ask: Can I get more money here than somewhere else? Will I have to pay more (submit to more invasions of my privacy or to more demands for changing my way of life)?'[5] Note also the conclusions of a study carried out in the U.S., in which recipients of public assistance were interviewed:

> Clients were in dire need, since the assistance allowance, originally set low, never caught up with the inflationary trend. They were, therefore, under strong pressure to conceal what slim resources they might have had and try to get a little more money from the agency, even if this required false statements. People under such deprived conditions tend to look upon government organizations as alien forces that must be tricked into yielding enough money for survival, and consequently some clients, although by no means all, tried to cheat. In fact, the situation in which recipients found themselves made honesty a luxury.[6]

It need hardly be added that 'impression management', whether of this or other kinds, is anathema to any kind of therapy calling for spontaneity on the part of the client. One can hardly be 'natural', so to speak, while concurrently pursuing ulterior ends.

Resentment Clients seeking interpersonal help were often angry and resentful as a result of their help-seeking experiences. It appears to us, however, that this was even more true of those in search of material assistance. The latter's feelings were manifested in different ways during treatment. Mrs Gore intentionally let the workers come to an 'empty house' on one occasion, instead of letting them know she was unable to keep her appointment. Mrs Denton, who in other respects seemed rather mild, described in clipped tones her last visit to the FWA: 'I never went back. I walked down the stairs and never said good-bye or thank you. I just walked down the stairs.' As with differences in relation to 'impression management', the greater resentment experienced by these clients was seemingly a by-product of situational factors.

Those in search of material assistance, we suggested earlier, sought to ingratiate themselves with the worker. To some extent, they did things they did not want to do in order to appear 'deserving'. Efforts of this type are apt to be stressful. More significantly, they are apt to generate feelings of self-disgust, which in time become converted into anger and resentment towards those 'responsible' for their self-contempt. Thus, it seems perfectly understandable why Mrs Denton, who felt she 'had lowered herself and still got nowhere', 'never said good-bye or thank you' to the worker. Processes of this kind were not evident among clients in search of inter-personal help nor would one typically expect them to be present. These individuals were not 'humbling' themselves and so were less susceptible to resentment-producing processes of the type noted.

Secondly, both sets of clients were resentful when they felt they were not trusted. But the misperceptions of those seeking material help seemingly had more devastating effects. The latter, we suspect, took the caseworker's actions as confirming the fact that, in the eyes of the worker, they were morally reprehensible. We are admittedly reading between the lines at this point, but it is a plausible supposition. Unlike their counterparts, these clients came to the agency burdened with a sense of shame. They felt they were begging and were fearful that they would be considered cadgers or unworthy for other reasons. Given this context, the tendency on the part of their workers to return, repeatedly, to the same line of questioning was perceived as a form of cross-examination, as an indication that they were not trusted. The worker's actions, in brief, fell upon an area that was already inflamed and in so doing evoked considerable resentment. To compound matters further, the less trusted these clients felt, presumably the more energy they devoted to ingratiating themselves—a process which, as already noted, had independent anger producing effects of its own.

Finally, a sizeable number of those seeking material assistance were aware that others had succeeded where they had failed and this angered them further:

> *Mrs Gore*: I know people who get help with their children's clothes at the National Assistance and then they go out every night in the pub drinking and leave their children alone at home. . . . That's what annoys me.

> *Mrs Denton*: If I didn't know that they helped with other people, it [not getting help] wouldn't have troubled me so much.

> *Mrs Small*: My sister said, 'My God, you don't expect that they are going to give you money at the FWA, do you! They are just there to talk to.' But I know differently. It's proved differently—there *are* people who get help, whereas I haven't received any and I'm afraid I'm very jealous of them.

Compared to those seeking interpersonal help, clients such as these seemed to have a wider knowledge of how other persons had fared at the FWA or other help-providing agencies. They knew (or at least felt they knew) how cases similar to theirs were handled, that is, whether the applicants had actually received material assistance or not. This does not seem particularly surprising. The act of giving or withholding material assistance is a clear-cut matter, relatively speaking, and as a result news about other people's help-seeking experiences is apt to circulate more freely. An individual may see for himself if a neighbour has been helped; the electricity may be turned on again, the rent may be paid, new clothes may be in evidence and so forth. Or he may receive information from acquaintances regarding the help-seeking experiences of those unbeknown to him. Or perhaps those who have earlier been to the agency will disclose what happened to them. However, the manner in which an agency deals with a marital or parent-child problem is less easily summarized. It is a more elusive and multi-faceted matter. The worker may do a great many different things, and it may be more difficult for the client to pigeon-hole and summarize—and thus discuss—what actually took place. Because of this, information about treatment processes and outcomes in such instances is probably more restricted, less widely dispersed. It is perhaps no accident that all of the clients cited in chapter four who came to the agency partly as a result of talking with ex-clients were persons in search of material, not interpersonal, help.

The upshot of the above is that those who came to the agency in the hope that members of their families would be 'straightened out'—and who were subsequently disappointed—were not in a position to conclude that they had been unfairly treated or deprived in some other way.[7] But this was less so of their counterparts; because the latter felt they knew what had happened to others, they felt deprived and in turn resentful. In this connection, Malcolm Ford's statement is very much to the point: 'Many social workers know very well that if they have not done so yet, they will have to cope one day with the question: "My next-door neighbour came here and you paid her rent arrears, so why won't you pay mine?"'[8]

The two points of contrast between the clients above with respect to impression-management and resentment, should not be taken as 'hard' fact. They are offered more in the way of suggestions. In comparing these two sets of clients, we have tended to overlook differences within each group, to say nothing of the fact that relevant data were sometimes lacking. Moreover, little heed was paid to moderating or counter influences. For example, those individuals who hoped to obtain material help expected their experiences to be painful and this very fact may have made their actual experiences less distressing than would otherwise have been the case. Notwithstanding, we believe the suggestions offered have good plausibility, if only because they are compatible with what is known of the behaviour and reactions of persons in comparable situations.

10

Towards more effective casework service

Much has been written about the process of social casework, but not from the viewpoint of the client. This book has offered a study that begins to correct this serious imbalance. Towards this end, sixty-one former clients of the Family Welfare Association were interviewed in an effort to learn something about their perceptions of, and reactions to, the services offered. It cannot be claimed that this study represents anything like a complete picture of casework services in operation. The clients studied were few in number and were drawn from one particular agency. Moreover, they were restricted in terms of their social characteristics. They were primarily working-class wives of British descent who came to the agency either for material assistance or for help in dealing with someone else. Whether our findings hold for other sub-groups of the working class population (e.g., different nationalities, husbands as well as wives) or for those who seek help for other problems (e.g., 'personal' rather than 'interpersonal' ones) remains to be seen.

Our study focused on two time periods—the pre-contact and contact phases of treatment. Concerning the former, we saw that inadequacies in the client's informal network generated a tendency to seek external help. In some instances our respondents lacked persons in whom they felt they could confide, while in others those who were available were for some reason considered unsuitable. Our findings strongly support Gurin's remarks that 'a person who goes for help with a personal problem is, in a sense, revealing at least two assumptions that he has made about his situation: first, that he is faced with a personal problem that distresses him; and second, that he cannot solve this problem by himself or by the help and advice of family and friends'.[1]

While the point was not fully developed, we suggested that an individual's interactions with friends and relatives—in addition to affecting the likelihood of his seeking professional help—will condition his later responses to treatment. For example, clients who questioned the discretion of friends were buoyed up by the confidentiality of the casework situation. Conversely, those who received supportive (but not instrumental) help from their network were relatively unmoved by the bolstering efforts of their workers. These processes (as well as those noted in other sections) can be taken to illustrate an important point that is all too frequently overlooked: client reactions to treatment may be affected by factors outside the awareness of workers and ones over which they have little control.

Before coming to the agency, few of our respondents had ever heard of the FWA; or if they had, they knew little about it. This being the case, referral agents played an especially important role. For one thing, they were responsible for bringing the agency to the clients' attention. But in addition, informal agents—and we are referring here primarily to friends and acquaintances who had earlier been clients themselves—tended to convey a very positive picture of the agency based on their own experience; these reports, in turn, led clients to feel assured that they would receive the particular kinds of help which they sought. In all likelihood, these influences would have been less significant if clients had been more familiar with agency operations. Formal agents were also responsible for fostering contact but in a somewhat different way. On some occasions, they took active steps to ensure that the respondent would actually go to the FWA, e.g., by arranging appointments. Had the respondent invariably been left 'on his own', we suspect that contact in certain instances might never have been established.

Both inadequacies in the client's network and the influence of referral agents played an important role in fostering contact with the agency. While we have not done so earlier, it might be useful consider these two influences conjointly. Presumably those who are troubled by problems and whose networks are grossly inadequate are apt to solicit professional help, even though they receive little, if any, 'push' from referral agents. Conversely, those whose networks are more adequate may require a more vigorous push from referral agents if contact is to be established.

Most of the analysis undertaken in our study centred on the interaction between worker and client. At this point, however, we shall present only a cursory review of our findings, as these have already been summarized in some detail at earlier points. Our respondents, it will be recalled, were differentiated both in terms of the kind of help they sought and their reactions to the service offered. These classifications produced four types of clients.

Those who sought help in dealing with someone else and were dissatisfied were treated by workers who were 'insight-oriented', and this very fact generated a series of misunderstandings. These clients assumed that their workers would share their views concerning problem-solving and when this did not turn out to be the case, they imputed erroneous meanings to their workers' activities—ones, incidentally, which friends and relatives, due to their own unsophistication, were unable to correct. For example, the clients concluded that the worker was not interested in them, did not trust them, lacked the authority to take appropriate action and so forth. By leading clients to become angered or resigned, these various imputations undermined the worker's efforts to help and served to drive the two parties further apart.

Clients who sought help of a similar kind but were satisfied encountered workers who employed a different treatment approach. The latter were less 'insight-oriented', supplying instead a type of therapy that might roughly be labelled 'supportive-directive'. As a result, these respondents were not subject to the kinds of misunderstandings encountered by those above. Significantly, however, it was not only the *absence* of strain and misunderstanding that accounted for their responsiveness. These clients were given ample opportunity to unburden themselves; they were emotionally supported by the worker's interest and concern; they were offered various suggestions and advice; and they were 'enlightened' in ways that were apparently perceived as comprehensible. Unfortunately, we know little about their earlier views concerning problem-solving. On the one hand, they may have been some-what different from those that were typically held by the dissatisfied clients whom we interviewed. On the other hand, similar views may have been shared by the two sets of clients. If the latter were so, the satisfaction experienced by these particular clients may have partially derived from the fact that the worker's approach in these instances was more com-patible with their notions as to how problems of their type should be dealt with.

Clients in search of material, rather than interpersonal, help were a good deal more resistant about coming to the agency. Moreover, if we are to make sense of their later reactions to treatment, we must thoroughly understand the source and nature of their antipathy to seeking help. These clients antici-pated that the treatment experience would be punishing. For one thing, they were ashamed of their financial dependency and to expose their plight to others would only increase their humiliation. Secondly, a sympathetic response was the very last thing they expected from the agency. It was anticipated that the worker would be harsh and abrupt; in all likelihood he would be contemptuous of their plight; and he might well imagine that they were only there to 'cadge' what they could get. There is not the slightest doubt that these individuals dreaded the prospect of becoming clients.

Let us first turn to those who had a favourable experience. Not only did they receive material assistance of some kind—this was of vital importance—but they were surprised, even shocked, to find that the process of soliciting material aid was a good deal less unpleasant than anticipated. But these were not the only considerations accounting for their satisfaction. On numerous occasions, they received not inconsiderable benefits from the supportive-directive approach that was utilized by these particular workers. In this respect they correspond closely to the satisfied clients earlier considered.

Significantly, those who were dissatisfied typically failed to obtain the help which they so desperately sought. But in addi-tion, they were characteristically treated by insight-oriented workers, and this fact generated a series of misunderstandings and severe aggravations similar to those earlier noted. These clients failed to understand what their workers were trying to do and sometimes reached conclusions that were devastating in their effects. Perhaps one example will suffice. At least several clients suspected that the worker's continuing exploration of their personal lives ultimately comprised efforts to 'catch them out'. Given their earlier sensitivities concerning such matters, not surprisingly, they became angry and resentful. Moreover, their interpretations, inaccurate though they were, decisively put an end to any therapeutic gains that might conceivably have been achieved.

This has, to some extent, been a study of certain effects of different treatment approaches (on clients in search of differing kinds of help). This, we might add, was in no sense planned. When we began the study, we knew little about the approaches utilized by different workers and we certainly had no thought of assessing their effectiveness.[2] As it turned out, however, the approaches employed were rather evenly divided between 'insight' and 'supportive-directive' and each was closely associated with different treatment outcomes (as judged by the client). This inevitably raises questions about the potential utility of the approaches employed and this in turn leads into matters concerned with social planning, casework practice, and research. In the remaining pages, several of these issues will be examined.

Let us first turn our attention to clients in search of material assistance. To offer clients, such as those studied, psychological help—without satisfying, and preferably at the start, their material needs—in our view utterly fails to come to grips with their problems. The persons we interviewed were desperately trying to survive. They were consumed with worry over debts, the possibility of an eviction, the cutting-off of their electricity, and it is absurd to expect that the urgency of their needs could be met by a non-material approach, whether this be a matter of offering insight, providing friendship, or the opportunity to unburden themselves to a sympathetic listener. Plainly put, these individuals were desperately in need of money (or its equivalent) and to offer them something else is to offer a suit of clothes to a drowning man.

In saying this, we are well aware that money is not a universal panacea. Economic difficulties have a way of precipitating non-economic ones and these may require help of an additional sort. In fact, in some instances (though probably few in number) the financial problem may constitute little more than a reflection of strains that are more psychological in nature, as for example the sexually frustrated husband whose resentment leads him to squander his wages, leaving little aside for food and rent. Presumably the offer of money in such instances would have little, if any, beneficial effect. However, in an over-all sense, the presence of these psychological complications, at least in our view, has had a deleterious effect on the social work profession in that it has drawn attention away from the underlying economic issues involved. In their pre-occupation with psychological matters, social workers have tended to develop an occupational blindness to economic realities.[3] Put somewhat differently, were they forced to exchange places with their clients, it is not unlikely that they would be beset by similar difficulties, their psychological sophistication notwithstanding.

The plight of those seeking material assistance derived in great part from a societal failure to provide adequate economic security and opportunity. To imagine that our respondents came to the FWA because they were 'indolent', 'opportunistic' or had a 'don't care' attitude would be purely delusionary. We are well aware, of course, that delusions of this sort are common and their persistence, in the face of so much evidence to the contrary, no doubt attests to the important functions they perform, enabling those who hold them, for example, to avoid taking action of any type. However, as far as our respondents are concerned, it is plain that they were doing their utmost to cope on their own and going to the agency was the very last thing they wanted to do.

Now, voluntary agencies like the FWA are obviously not equipped to deal with the economic casualties of an entire social system. For example, they are unable to provide jobs for the unemployed or to raise the technological competence of those who are currently unskilled. As a matter of fact, they are even unable to provide fully for the needs of those whom they might wish to accept as clients and not refer to other social agencies. On many occasions the modesty of the help offered by the FWA can only comprise partial and temporary solutions at best. It is very clear that only substantial changes in our social structure can prevent situations of the type described in our study from regularly recurring in the future. Whether this ultimately entails more adequate benefits, a negative income tax, or changes more fundamental in character is beyond the scope of our study and comprises a problem for those in social administration, public finance, political sociology and related fields. The only point we wish to make is that the action taken must inevitably be social or collective in nature. To proceed in any other manner is analogous to attacking typhoid by offering medical care to the afflicted while leaving the source of the contagion—polluted water supplies—untouched.

Clearly, the kinds of changes required will not be instituted overnight. In the meantime, workers such as those at the FWA will be in the unenviable position of having to decide which of their clientele are to receive material assistance from the sources the FWA 'controls'. While this is ultimately a matter for the particular practitioners involved (and relevant committees), our study has produced several tangential suggestions which should prove helpful. Above all, our data suggest that workers should immediately take cognizance of the client's desire for financial help, perhaps by bringing his wishes out into the open. Hopefully too the worker will indicate as soon as possible what he is in a position to do for the client, either psychologically or materially. Procedures of this type would undoubtedly ease the client's tensions and anxieties. In so doing, they might well lead him to become more amenable to psychological help and curb his tendencies to ingratiate himself with the worker, with all the destructive consequences that this can entail.

In at least one important sense, problems that are essentially economic in nature present few theoretical issues for practitioners: the solutions, at least the long term ones, are clearly indicated. The situation is quite otherwise, however, for those whose problems are more 'psychological' or 'interpersonal'. At this point we simply do not know which of various problem-solving approaches holds out most promise for persons of working-class background—whether it be those seen in this study or some other such as a socio-behavioural approach. No doubt there are some who would consider such matters irrelevant. They might well hold that environmental reforms will lead to the elimination of both economic *and* non-economic difficulties. In this we agree but only partly. Social change in the form of better schools, more adequate housing, training in the use of leisure time and so forth would undoubtedly diminish the interpersonal strains that arise in the lives of working class people. Unfortunately, however, a certain residue of interpersonal strain is bound to remain with us, even under improved conditions. In this connection, one need only consider those who are currently leading comfortable and affluent lives. No one has suggested, at least to our knowledge, that they are in any sense immune from the non-financial strains depicted in our study.

Our remarks above concerning the problematic effects of different treatment approaches might seem incompatible with the results of our study. That is, we saw very clearly that the persons whom we interviewed profited greatly (at least in their judgment) from a supportive-directive approach but gained little, if anything, from an insight-oriented one. It might be concluded from this that the former should be espoused and the latter abandoned. Such a conclusion, one might add, would be wholly compatible with certain tendencies—or, more accurately, ideological upheavals—that are currently sweeping the mental health profession. Of late, there has been a growing disenchantment with insight-oriented procedures. As one observer puts it, '. . . within many social work circles, the concept of the unconscious and its impact on human behaviour has become a dirty word'.[4] In its more radical form, this disillusionment has led some to advocate the wholesale abandonment of insight-oriented procedures for persons of working class background. We are completely unsympathetic with prescriptions of this type, for, if nothing else, they assume answers to questions about which we currently know very little. In the following we shall try to make our meaning clear.

To begin with, not a great deal is known about the effects of other (i.e., non-insight-oriented) approaches on persons of working-class background and most notably their long-term effects. This is certainly so as far as supportive-directive procedures are concerned. It is conceivable that help of this description may turn out to be limited, both in terms of its durability and its implications for problem-solving in other areas. For one thing, those who are treated by this method may find that the results achieved are temporary in nature; strains to which they are subject, though 'solved' at one point, may constantly reappear in their lives. Perhaps, too, the effects of a supportive-directive approach will be relatively specific in the sense that they will not enable those treated either to prevent or cope more effectively with difficulties arising in *other areas* of their lives.

Unlike insight-oriented therapy which seeks in a sense to keep an individual on course by altering his gyroscope, supportive-directive therapy, it seems to us, seeks to attain the same end by constantly shoring the individual up—primarily by supplying external bolstering of some type.

The upshot of these differences is that those who are treated by supportive-directive methods may be in need of constant 'repairs' if we focus on their lifetime, rather than more limited segments of time. As a matter of fact, if we take a long-range view of matters and compare them to those receiving insight-oriented therapy, they may require more, rather than less, professional help—and we are taking into account the larger initial investment of time required by insight-oriented procedures. It is ironic that what is currently envisioned as 'short-term' treatment, when placed on a different time scale, may turn out to be 'long-term'. We do not know the answers to these questions, but they clearly call for longitudinal studies centring on the long-term effects of a supportive-directive approach. At the very least, they provide warning that such an approach cannot unthinkingly be advocated on the basis that it saves professional time.[5]

Much of our study has been concerned with insight-oriented procedures, and our findings raise pointed questions concerning their potential utility. Above all, an approach of this type, our data strongly suggest, will prove ineffective unless clients first acquire some understanding of the assumptions underlying its use. Thus, the critical question becomes: can working-class clients be 'resocialized' or re-educated to the views of their workers? (Assuming agreement on this as a desirable aim.) One might tackle this issue by immediately offering clients instruction of some type, for example, through the therapist (or a surrogate) familiarizing them with the assumptions underlying their approach. Several attempts have already been made along these lines.[6]

However, a complementary approach—and one which we see as more productive in the long run—would involve prior efforts to learn more about the views of those who would on the former assumption have to be 're-educated'. We already know, for example, that working class clients tend to attribute their difficulties to external conditions, are not introspectively inclined, and expect the worker to play an active part in solving their problems. Our own findings in which working-class clients were depicted as having, in varying degrees, a unicausal moralistic-suppressive approach carry these notions a little further. However, as researchers, we can ill afford to stop at this point. We need to obtain a more adequate picture of working-class views and their prevalence within different sub-groups of the working-class population. In addition, we need to learn more about the source of these views, how embedded they are and what functions they serve in the various strands of working-class life. Unless issues of this type are explored in some detail, any efforts to 're-socialize' clients may well founder. An apt warning is provided by the results of a mental health study carried out in a Canadian area, in which members of the local population served as subjects. The researchers hoped to increase the villagers' understanding of mental illness, as currently conceived by mental health professionals. With this end in view, they undertook an educational campaign. Unfortunately, however, the campaign failed, largely because the investigators, at the inception of the study, failed to appreciate certain of the villagers' implicit conceptions about behaviour which ultimately shaped their beliefs about mental illness.[7]

Until more is known about the nature and source of the problem-solving views held by working-class people, nothing definite can be said about the likelihood of successfully 'resocializing' them. This, however, need not prevent us from making certain predictions. If it should turn out that working-class people espouse views like those of the dissatisfied clients we interviewed—and some undoubtedly will—we are very doubtful that workers (or their surrogates) would have much success in fundamentally altering their conceptions, even assuming extensive instruction and discussion. In effect, we visualize the cognitive gap between worker and client as being essentially unbridgeable in certain instances. Perhaps this will strike the reader as an overly extreme view, and he might well contend that such assumptions have not been put to the test, at least in our study. In this we would have to agree. From what we know, the FWA workers in our study made few efforts to familiarize their clients with the assumptions underlying their approach, and it is not inconceivable that if they had, they might have had some success.

In the final analysis, our views concerning the intractability of client viewpoints derive from certain considerations that heretofore have remained unexpressed. Specifically, our views are based not only on the particular behavioural conceptions revealed by our clients. They derive also from an underlying suspicion that the conceptual differences between workers and clients are, in some instances, even more basic than those dealt with in our study—in fact, not wholly unlike the differences that separate the practitioners of Western medicine from the non-literate populations they hope to serve.[8] Perhaps a few examples will clarify what we have in mind. (In this, as in other parts of the book where we draw attention to social class differences, we run the risk of seeming to describe one class in terms which denote its apparent failure to resemble the other. It is not, of course, our intention to depict working-class people as somehow 'incomplete' middle-class people, or to suggest that their views are in some way 'irrational'. Many of the attitudes we depict as 'working-class' are explicable as responses to an environment, experienced through the generations as deeply intractable.)

To begin with, it seems probable that working-class people do not readily think in interactional terms—for example, that their partner's behaviour is in some measure a response to their own.[9] It also seems unlikely that behaviour is seen in cultural terms—that is, as an expression of behavioural patterns that have been unthinkingly assimilated over the years in contrast to behaviour that is motivated by wilful intent. We query also whether working-class people conceive of behaviour in inter-dependent terms—whether given acts, for example, are viewed as compensations for or by-products of something else. Finally, to 'explain' the behaviour of others—a phenomenon in which all of us are constantly engaged—is to become involved in a complex process of drawing inferences. As Kinglsey Davis points out, 'the essential feature of communication is that one person infers from the behaviour of another (whether speech, gesture, or posture) what idea or feeling the other is trying to convey. He then reacts not to the behaviour as such but to the inferred idea or feeling.'[10] In this connection, it seems probable that working-class people do not see themselves as involved in a process of this type. Instead, they may mentally fuse the event and the explanation offered. In sum, it is questions such as these that ultimately explain our scepticism concerning the resocial-ization of certain clients.[11]

As we have tried to make plain throughout our study, not all working-class persons share the same views, and what holds for some will not hold for others. More specifically, the cognitive gap between worker and client will assuredly be less vast in certain instances, and when this is the case the worker (or a surrogate) may well have more success in his resocializing efforts. In this connection, the work of Orne and Wender is very relevant.[12] Like ourselves, they are concerned with the source of the working-class person's 'inappropriate' treatment expectations, but they visualize these as deriving from sources other than those to which we have attended, or at least paid substantial attention. In their view, the working-class person's expectations stem from his earlier experiences with other professionals, notably physicians. They point out that a client, in consulting a physician, describes his difficulties and then waits for a solution, either in the form of advice or treatment prescription. Psychotherapy, on the other hand, calls for interaction of an entirely different sort and one for which they are ill prepared by dint of these earlier encounters. As yet, we do not know to what extent confounding factors of the type noted derive from the sources suggested. However, if it should turn out that contact with physicians does play a large role in shaping subsequent therapeutic expectations (in contrast to influences that are more pervasive or 'cultural'), we might well expect that significant modifications in outlook would be possible. In sum—and this is to repeat what we said before—if we are going to try to 'resocialize' clients, we must first learn more about the source and nature of the views they currently hold.

A final word about insight-oriented therapy should be added. Our discussion up to this point has been completely taken up with issues centring on the resocialization of clients—solely because we have concluded, on the basis of our study, that unless clients understand what their workers are about, an approach of this type is bound to fail. This, however, says nothing about the effects of such an approach if and when clients *are* successfully resocialized. It may or may not prove effective—these are clearly questions for future research, yet ones that are best postponed until issues that are logically prior are resolved or at least explored.

It is a foregone conclusion that investigation of the issues outlined (and others) will not produce unambiguous results. That is, it will not indicate that one form of treatment—be it insight-oriented or supportive-directive—is to be preferred for clients of all description. In this connection, we may well discover that only certain clients can be resocialized and among these that only certain ones can benefit from an insight-oriented approach. Similar remarks can be made of a supportive-directive approach. We may find that in certain instances its effects are temporary while in others they are more lasting, and when the latter is the case it may become the preferred form of treatment. To say this is merely to repeat what we said in the introduction—that the essential task of the researcher is to discover what forms of treatment are most appropriate for clients of different description. These are issues that will occupy us for some time to come. They are also ones which clients, acting as informants, can help us to solve.

Appendices

Appendix I Sample letter to client from Family Welfare Association

Family Welfare Association Central Office: Denison House
296 Vauxhall Bridge Road SW1

Dear . . .

I am writing to you because you have recently had some contact with one of our social workers. The Family Welfare Association is interested in improving the service it gives to people, and we are at present co-operating with two independent research workers from the London School of Economics in a study of the opinions and views of those who have used our services. I am, therefore, writing to ask if you would help us by permitting a research worker to interview you in your home to obtain your views about our service.

Any information you provide will be treated in strictest confidence. Your name will not be used in any way, nor will anyone at the FWA or anywhere else be able to connect your name with anything you have said. It is only in this way that we can hope to obtain frank answers from the persons interviewed.

A fee of £1 will be offered in return for your time and co-operation and will be paid when the interview takes place. The interviewer will probably be in your area the week of ——————————, and she would like to drop by to arrange a time for the interview. If I do not hear from you to the contrary by —————————— I shall assume that you would like the interviewer to call.

Thanking you in anticipation.

Yours sincerely,

(Miss) M. P. Daniel,
Head of Social Work Department

Appendix 2 Previous helpers as a frame of reference for appraising the worker

Since the FWA is one of the largest training agencies in England, some of its clients are treated by student social workers undertaking fieldwork training in the FWA. When students complete their placement, their clients must necessarily be transferred to permanent members of the casework staff. This inevitably means that there are clients who must be transferred to different workers during the course of their treatment—which happened to some of those we studied. We are not concerned with all of the complexities this may entail, but with only one facet of the situation—namely, that the client's earlier helping experiences may provide a benchmark or a point of reference in terms of which later ones are judged. An apt illustration is provided by the case of Mrs Brain, who was treated by three different workers. The first two workers offered a good deal of practical, supportive help—which was immensely appreciated. The third worker, however, believed (she was interviewed by us) that the client would ultimately derive more benefit if less were done for her, so-to-speak, in the way of practical services. The processes by which favourable expectations are built up in a client's mind and then used as a later point of reference are clearly revealed in the client's account of her experiences:

> All three of these ladies came to see me. The first one was very, very nice—an ordinary, everyday person. She'd come in, sit down, and make herself at home. Even if your place wasn't 100 per cent, you didn't have to feel embarrassed or anything. She'd just say, 'Just leave the dishes—sit down and rest yourself.' She never made a fuss or anything. When I found out I was having another baby, I was terribly upset. She said that I may not want the baby now but when it came I would feel good about it. When I was having the baby she helped me to get

some baby clothes and some blankets. And she got me a gas
cooker she did, and a pram. Oh, she was very helpful. It was a
good thing that I had someone like her at the time to come and
see me. . . . The second lady was very nice, too. She was
lovely she was. Very good friends we were. She was really
very, very kind to me.

But I just couldn't get on with the third lady—there was no
hard feelings or anything. She was a very pleasant sort of
person, but I don't think she had the go in her for that kind of
job. She was the sort of person where you have to ask, 'Well,
will you do this or will you do that or can you get me
anything?' Well, I mean people in need shouldn't have to be
so blunt about it. She should understand these things, at least
that's my opinion. They should understand why she's there—
to get in touch with these people and to try to help us. She
never asked me even at Christmas if there was something I
needed for the children, like the other ladies did. I mean both
Miss G and Miss L told me, that's what they're there for—to
find out these things and if people are in difficulties, they're
there to help them.

I felt this lady didn't understand. You had to put the words
in her mouth if you wanted her to get you anything or do
anything for you. You had to say, 'Will you get it? Will you
go there? Will you ask them for it?' Well I mean this is not the
sort of person you need in the predicament I'm in—you need
a person who'll listen to your problem and say, 'Right, I'll see
what I can do about it.' I can honestly say that the other two
were very, very good and very helpful. But seeing this one was
a waste of everyone's time.

There are several comments worth making regarding comparison
processes of the type noted. For one thing, it is important to recognize
that these processes operate within a variety of contexts. That is,
clients who compared their current workers with a predecessor (or
predecessors) in the same agency were not the only ones who reacted
to their current helpers in terms of someone else. In the course of our
study we had frequent occasion to note who the 'someone else'
was and how he served as a benchmark or point of reference for
the client's later experiences. For example, some of our clients
reacted to their workers partially in terms of earlier help-seeking
encounters with friends and relatives. Several respondents were
very pleased to find that their transactions with the workers were
confidential, unlike those with certain members of their network.
Others were unimpressed with the worker partly because the help
provided by the network was considered equally, or more, effective.

Not infrequently, the worker at the FWA was compared with other professionals—child welfare workers, probation officers, psychiatrists, employees of the NAB and Social Security and so forth. As we have seen, Mrs Lawton, who had matrimonial problems, was confused and disheartened by the worker's non-directive approach to her difficulties. This was partially a function of her preceding experiences at another family agency, where the particular worker with whom she dealt had 'really given her the answers' and told her what she should do about her situation. In sum, Mrs Brain's tendency (she was quoted above) to appraise her third worker at the FWA in terms of the preceding two constitutes merely one instance of a general comparison-making process.

The question arises as to whether social workers are aware of the processes discussed—ones which, as we have seen, help to account for the client's reactions during treatment. It is our suspicion that they are apt to be very sensitive about possible intra-agency comparisons that are made by the client, but are relatively unaware of ones involving *outsiders* and agency personnel. In this connection, the third worker to deal with Mrs Brain was completely cognizant of what was going on: she fully recognized that the client would appraise her in terms of her earlier help at the FWA and she was not the least bit surprised that the client was initially 'cool' or non-responsive to her methods. A similar awareness was revealed by other workers who were involved in agency transfers. At the same time, the workers whom we interviewed (and this includes those who were not involved in transfers) evidenced little awareness of similar processes operating outside the agency. In this connection, we explicitly asked the workers whether their clients, before coming to the agency, ever discussed their difficulties with friends or relatives and if so how the clients reacted to any help that was offered. The workers were able to supply hardly any information on these matters. In many instances, the client's interaction with informal helpers had never been considered, presumably because it was felt to be irrelevant. Our data suggest, however, that it (as well as experiences with other professionals) is not irrelevant but significantly affects the client's valuation of the worker. A fuller understanding of these processes, on the part of the caseworker, would presumably enable him to increase the effectiveness of his practice.

Appendix 3 The non-assimilation of professional norms

Much of our attention in the current study has centred around dissatisfied clients, particularly the sources of their dissatisfaction. By and large we viewed their discontent as stemming from the fact that they and their workers had different ways of thinking about and coping with personal problems. Specifically, the clients interviewed tended to view their problems as stemming from the other party; moreover, they felt that they could only be solved if coercion were brought to bear on the culprit. The social workers, on the other hand, had a more sophisticated view of the causes involved and gave high priority to the therapeutic effects of 'self-awareness'. In brief, the two parties had different cognitive orientations to problem-solving.

There are indications, however, that another and distinctly different type of barrier separated the two parties. Specifically, professionals—whether they be doctors, lawyers or social workers—tend to have certain notions concerning the ways in which professional-client relationships should be structured. Scattered remarks in our interviews, however, suggest that clients were not always aware of these norms; or if they were aware of them that they did not always accept them. In the following we shall briefly outline certain of the basic norms adhered to (or, at least, annunciated) by professionals and then discuss some client reactions to them.[1]

1 According to the normative structure, the professional's overriding aim should be to help the client. This purpose should very definitely take precedence over competing aims, e.g., the desire for money, influence, power, or acclaim—interests that are permitted to claim the full attention of those involved in other occupational pursuits. Ideally, according to Wilensky and Lebeaux, the professional should be 'selfless'—he should keep personal and commercial interests subordinated to the client's needs.[2]

If the professional is to be maximally effective, it is expected that he will keep his personal feelings about the client from interfering with treatment. He cannot afford to idealize the patient or to give free rein to hostile reactions. Our interview material indicates, however, that clients did not always visualize or conceive of their workers in terms of these norms. They did not invariably consider them emotionally 'neutral' and by implication as primarily service-oriented. For example, we earlier noted at some length that clients in search of material assistance tended to expect punitive responses from the worker and in some instances to be viewed with contempt. Moreover, a number of those in search of interpersonal help concluded that their workers were *not* really interested in helping them. (These clients, it will be recalled, were trying to explain why their workers were not dealing with their problems in ways which they, the clients, considered appropriate.) Both of these illustrations suggest an unfamiliarity on the part of clients with the professional's service-oriented norms, or at least the primacy assigned to them by professionals.

All of this is not to say that professionals will invariably succeed in living up to these norms: in some instances, personal and 'inappropriate' emotions will presumably filter into the treatment situation; moreover, on other occasions, the professional's service-oriented ideals may be diluted by other considerations.[3] However, this discrepancy between the ideal and the actual (which is a common characteristic of everyday life) cannot fully explain the reactions of certain clients. In our view, their reactions were partially a by-product of the fact that the existence of the norms was unknown to them.

2   The professional (at least in his view) is entitled to explore intimate aspects of the client's life, on the basis that any relevant information, no matter how private, must be revealed if the help offered is to be effective. In return for the free access to information, the professional guarantees that any information obtained will be held in strict confidence and not misused for private gain. Our interview material suggests, however, that this contractual exchange, which is often taken for granted by professionals, was not necessarily taken for granted by clients. In some instances, the particular questions which the worker asked led him to be viewed as 'nosey', someone who was merely interested in gossip, or someone who was trying to pique or annoy the client. Occasionally, the client's reactions were a good deal stronger. At least several clients were offended and incensed when the worker questioned them about their relations (sexual or otherwise) with their spouses. Mrs Wilson, for example, felt the worker had 'no right' to ask questions of this

type—ones which even her friends and family would not ask. In addition to not accepting the legitimacy of the worker's line of questioning, a number of clients—and we have already dealt with this—were unfamiliar with the worker's norms concerning the confidentiality of information disclosed. In brief, professional norms of the type described were apparently not part of the clients' thinking, at least not always.

3 The interaction between client and practitioner, according to the professional's norms, should be limited to the matter at hand, to the client's difficulties. In Parsons' terms, the relationship should be 'functionally specific', rather than 'diffuse' as in friendships. Wilensky and Lebeaux observe in their discussion of professional behaviour, 'if personal information is sought, it is information relevant to the performance of the technical task [the solution of the problem]; if rapport must be established, it is rapport for a purpose . . . the worker typically does not "make friends" with the client. He does not reveal his personal life, entertain the client socially in his home, or visit with the client on a social basis.'[4]

We had the impression, however, that in some instances clients had a decidedly less restricted view of the relationship. Many of their remarks were reminiscent of someone describing a friendship. For example, clients sometimes referred to their interviews as 'chats'; one client explicitly likened them to 'gabbing with someone in a pub'.[5] Another indication that the relationship was perceived in friendship terms is suggested by various expressions of reciprocity and indebtedness. Clients were sometimes anxious to 'repay' the worker for all he had done; they felt indebted and above all were anxious not to offend him in any way. Sentiments of this type are notably characteristic of diffuse relationships (friendships). In at least one instance, the client was very explicit in her efforts to befriend the worker. She invited the worker to her home for a cup of tea and was very surprised that the worker declined, on the basis that too much intimacy would be bad for the treatment relationship. In more general terms, a number of observers have pointed out that working class people tend to personalize relationships. For example, Miller and Riessman remark that 'in the bureaucratic situation, the worker . . . tends to think of himself as relating to people, not to roles and invisible organizational structure'.[6] The interview material we have discussed would appear to reflect tendencies of this nature.

The material outlined above raises a number of questions which are worth further investigation. For example, to what extent are working-class people unaware of the norms which regulate professional behaviour?[7] Is their non-awareness confined to *certain* professional encounters, for example those with mental health therapists, or does it extend to encounters with lawyers, doctors and other professionals as well? To what extent and in what ways does a non-awareness (or non-acceptance) of professional norms interfere with the professional's efforts to be helpful? What is the most feasible way of familiarizing clients with the professional's norms, assuming such a course is called for?

Appendix 4   Mrs Mountford

As an illustration of the kind of material we collected we reproduce the major part of our research interview with one of the former clients, Mrs Mountford. This is preceded by some details about her background. As we stated in the main text of the book we collected background information on all respondents.

Mrs Mountford was born in 1938 in London, where she has spent all her life. She was one of seven children, and she attended a secondary modern school, leaving at the age of fifteen. Like her husband who left school at sixteen she obtained no school leaving qualification. Before marriage she worked as a wages clerk. She now has six children: four boys (of eleven, seven, six and four years) and two girls (of three and two years). One of her sisters lives with her, but apart from this she is relatively isolated from her family. Her mother died some years ago, and she sees her other sister once or twice a month. She has one friend to whom she feels very close. This friend lives in the same street and they see each other every day.

The interview

Now could you tell me a little bit about the difficulties which first led you to go to the FWA? Yes, I had a sterilization operation after my last child, because they didn't want me to have any more, and afterwards I had one or two complications, and my husband had to stop away from work. Well, he was self-employed at the time which meant that he wasn't doing any work, so he didn't get any pay, no sick pay or anything like that. You know, sometimes some employers make concessions, and then it's been known they give you half pay . . . because he was self-employed, there was no chance of this. And so, we had a little bit of savings in the bank, and that sort of kept us going. But of course as that got dwindled down, we got behind with one or two things, mostly the rent. I think by the time we finished it was about £70. And they were going to take us to court, and try and evict us sort of thing. And we got in touch with the FWA through someone that my husband knew, a friend at work, he happened to be talking about the difficulties, and explained it to him.

How long had this been going on, Mrs Mountford? From the beginning of your illness, or . . . Well, I should say it was seven months, it was gradually getting worse, you know. And because he was self-employed, we didn't think that he could go to the Public Assistance, because he hadn't paid any stamps. That would have been a £1 a week out of our money, and we just couldn't afford it. Well we found out afterwards that he could have gone there, and probably could have got some sort of help. Well, altogether, I think it was about from November when I had the operation, I suppose from the January to the August, I believe, when we first got in touch with the FWA.

So it really started in November when you first had the operation? Yes. *And through the winter and the spring . . .* Yes, until August.

And was your husband not working all that time? No, he worked on and off, you know, when he could go. But when he got the contracts, things would happen that he couldn't go to work, then he'd lose a contract and things like that. It was a vicious circle of circumstances, really. As soon as he got something worked out, something else would happen here, and he wouldn't be able to do it, sort of thing.

Now, have you ever been in this sort of position before? No, this is the first time.

How much were you worried by this? Oh, terribly. I didn't mind, they cut our electricity off, the gas wasn't anything because it was meter, you know. But we hadn't been able to pay our electricity bill, and they disconnected that. I wasn't worrying about all the people, knocking on the door saying you owe me this; it was the rent, really. If it had just been my husband and I and just one child, we could have said, well that's too bad, we'll have to . . . but you can't, not with six children. You cannot get unfurnished accommodation, and furnished would be absolutely out of the question, it would be far too expensive. And I really was very worried, and I didn't know what was keeping me awake at night, and I got very depressed, you know. I was depressed anyway after the illness I had had. And it made me a bit more emotional, I think, because of that. And it was an awful strain, one way and another. But, I mean it was very worrying. I didn't care about anything else. It was the fact that we had nowhere to live, you know, what would we do, sort of thing.

Before you went to the FWA, did any of your friends and relatives know about the difficulties? Friends did, yes, especially when we had the electricity cut off, and they ran a cable for us, next door but one, you know. I was very friendly with her at the time, and they ran a cable thing from their front room window, so that we could have at least a light, in that room only, and the television; that was the only place we had light, nowhere else. And that was a help, mostly for the children. I didn't care, but they'd come home from school every evening, and nothing to do, no lights just candles. Very depressing, it sort of made the situation a bit more bleak.

What about your family, did anyone in the family know? My family knew that we went out to work, my mother and father were very good, and my mother used to send down tins of this and that because tins that are out of shape go to the employees at reduced prices. My father was very good. But I mean, they're buying their own house sort of thing, and they just had central heating put in, and one thing and another; we couldn't expect too much because I mean, although they've got a good income, it's all spoken for more or less.

But you were able to talk to them about the problem, you let them know what was going on? Not all of it, no, to a certain extent they knew, but we didn't tell them that we were so far in arrears with the rent and everything else.

Did you have any special reasons for not telling them? Yes, I think we were ashamed, it was just one of those things, we just didn't like to. In case they felt obligated to help us.

So you felt that if they knew all about it they would want to get you out as best they could? Probably, yes, and we had no hope of paying them back, not that time, it would just have got us more and more into debt, sort of thing. And as I say, I don't really think that they had that much money, not just to give you, just like that.

What about your sister, did you talk to her about it? No, again, we didn't. She knew we weren't doing too good, because my husband was out of work, but she didn't really know the extent of it. No.

What about your other sister, did you talk to her about it? No, I can't really say that I had. I'm not the sort of a person, you know, I believe that what goes on in my house is my and my husband's business only, you know. I'm not one to disclose anything.

No, it's just that some people feel differently. . . . Well, yes like my friend, now she'll tell me everything that goes on down her place, whereas I don't.

Now before you went to the FWA, did you try to get help from anywhere else? We didn't know anywhere else we could get help from.

Well, you mentioned the assistance? Well, we thought about it, but as I said, we were under the impression that it was all based on the National Insurance Scheme, and we just didn't think that it was possible, because as I say, my husband being self-employed, he was really behind with his national health stamps, and we didn't think that it was possible. Had we gone somewhere, or even if I'd spoken probably with our Health Visitor—because she was brought in when the court case come up—we might have got somewhere.

You would be seeing the Health Visitor because of the small children? Yes, that's right.

She was coming to see you or you saw her? I saw her at different times.

And did she say anything? No, because I didn't think she could help in that way sort of thing. I knew they could help as regards children being ill, but I didn't think she would be able to help in the way that we were in arrears and that she could do anything towards it.

So she didn't really know about this. No, she found out since, and she said, if only you'd said, we probably could have done something to help you, or got in touch with someone. But again, you see, this is all we found out afterwards; if only we'd known at the time.

Now, what led you to go to the FWA, how did you know about it? My husband was talking about something with a workman, all in a café together, and he happened to say that we were in a bit of a state because he was out of work and they were going to take us to court to evict us. And, I don't think he was a close friend, he was just someone that worked on the site with him. 'And you know', he said, 'well, I got into trouble once.' I think it was insurance stamps he was in bother with, and he said 'somebody put me on to this Family Welfare because my wife was very worried about it.' And this is all recommendation. His wife had spoken to somebody at her work, who had told her to get in touch with them, and they helped them out, so he said why don't you try, to my husband, and he said, you know, they probably could do something for you.

So it was somebody who recommended you to the FWA? Yes.

What did they say about them, can you recall what impression you had? Well, I don't know, I never saw the person. All I know is they said to my husband 'why don't you try the FWA'. They didn't know the address, they thought it would probably be in the phone book, you know, and they said, they might be able to help you. That as far as I know was all that was said. I don't know exactly. And he did say that they helped. . . .

So you didn't really have any idea apart from what this friend of your husband's had mentioned, you didn't know anybody else who'd been? No.

Now, this is a bit of a difficult question, but presumably you talked it over with you husband, and wondered whether to go, or not to go. Can you think back and recall what you expected it was going to be like before you went? Well, actually they came to us. And, well, I rather expected, sort of thing, for someone to come here, ask exactly what was wrong, and you could tell them. And then I quite expected them to rather give us a ticking off. And say, well now, how did you get in this state, in your position you should know better, and things like that, you know.

So you thought they'd probably be a bit disapproving? Well, although I didn't think that they wouldn't be helpful, they would help in what way they could, but I still thought that they would disapprove, rather strongly, sort of thing. And I was quite surprised when he did come, a very nice person.

What did you expect that they would do to help you? I hadn't any idea. I didn't think that they would be able to advance me a sum of money, not such a large sum.

So you didn't really think that they would come up with the cash? No, not really. I thought that perhaps maybe they would be able to get in touch with the Council and perhaps talk to them, although they knew of the circumstances, they'd given us plenty of time, sort of thing, but we just couldn't manage it. And I thought perhaps they would be able to get in touch with them, and come to some arrangement for us, in which we'd carry on paying our normal rent, and perhaps pay, you know, a £1 a week more, or something like that.

So you thought that they might be able to negotiate with them? Whereas we couldn't. That's right. I thought that because they were the FWA, and they would probably be able to talk to the landlord and explain the circumstances, and maybe get some more time, more than what we could.

Now, I'd like to ask you a bit about your actual experiences at the FWA. To begin with, what happened when you first made contact with them? Well, we wrote a letter first, and explained to them, and we received a letter back, stating that they understood how terribly worried we must be on the matter, and that they would be sending someone along, giving us a date and the time which the person would call. And that's what they did. And the young man, I fully expected to see a middle-aged woman.

You expected to see a woman? A very young man, really, he didn't look much older than my husband you know, came and saw us. And he was terribly nice, very understanding. As if it was all his fault. He was so apologetic and so sorry. But so terribly understanding, you know, to have someone who appeared genuinely to feel sorry for the predicament you was in. It was like ointment on a wound or something, you know, it was so soothing. I thought they was going to disapprove, or something, they're not going to like us, and they're bound to read us the riot act, you know first. But he really was good, sort of thing.

What sort of things did you talk about first, you'd obviously written a lot of it in the letter? Yes, when he came here, he asked to see all the books and the people to whom we owed money, or with whom we had accounts, such as insurances and hire purchase and all that, and then he made a list of all the people with whom we owed money to, and then he made a few suggestions as to how we should budget out money in order to pay these people. We should cut down and pay them the minimum, therefore showing that we are paying them, but not ignoring them, but also not spending large amounts out at a time. And then after that he asked us about our family, and my parents, and my husband's parents, and how we'd known each other before we were married, when we were married, and what our life together was like, how we got on together, what my feelings were since I had the sterilization, mostly about family life, you know, what did we think of the house, and the children, and what were we like together as a family, were we close, you know, such things.

So you talked, as well as talking about the actual practical problems, you talked a lot about each other and the family and the children. That's right, yes.

Now what sort of a person was this man who came to see you? As I said, he was very nice, extremely so, you know. I expected it would be somebody a lot older than what he was, and as I said, he was very sympathetic, sort of thing, which seemed to make the whole thing far easier, after you'd spoken to him, because he was so sympathetic.

This is what I was going to ask next. What was it like talking to him about these things? Very easy, yes. Very easy, you didn't feel embarrassed telling him the whole story. I mean, he was told everything, all the brutal facts and everything. But you felt no shame at telling him or anything like that.

Now, what did he think should be done? You've covered a bit what he actually did, like making a list of the debts. And paying off bit by bit. Did he have any other suggestions, or did he do anything else? It was mostly advice, he said he couldn't possibly offer such a large amount of cash which we needed to pay up the rent arrears. And that was the only one that we were really desperately worried about. The only one which we considered important enough to be cleared up there and then. But he said he was in touch with the Council, which is what we really wanted, and either we could come to some arrangement, or see what suggestions they had to help us out, of being evicted, and the court case and everything else. And most of it was just advice, as I say. As regards the bills he suggested that we cut them down, and we pay each of them a small amount rather than a large amount, and the rest. . . . The first time he came to see us he said he would get in touch with the Council to find out just what could be done, you know, in order to put off the court case and the eviction.

And did he manage to do this? Yes, he got in touch with them and they had case meetings, I believe they call it, in which was the people that were involved with us, such as the person on the behalf of the Housing Minister that comes to see cases like ours, and the Headmaster of the school, and a teacher who had been at school a long time and had taught my husband when he was at school. And they knew our children from the school, and also the Health Visitor, that had known me from a baby clinic and the children as well, and the School Care Committee Officer, I believe, that deals with free meals and, you know.

So they all got in? Yes, and they had a big meeting, and one or two others, I think, people from the Council.

And the worker from the FWA? Oh yes, he was there as well. And he put our case to them, explained everything to them, and the Council suggested therefore they were willing to help us. When we went to court, we would be told what we owed, and asked if there was any way in which we could pay these arrears, and they suggested that my husband say he would resume paying the normal rent plus so much a week off these arrears. And they suggested as I said, that he make these suggestions when he went to court, and that some arrangement would be made between my husband and the judge, you know, as to what could be done about this, which is what they did. Although it wasn't quite as easy as we were told it would happen. They said that we would be asked to make a suggestion, and that we would come to some arrangement with the court itself. This wasn't actually so. They wanted immediate possession, that was the first thing they stood up for, and they didn't seem as if they were prepared; that was the barrister for WCC. He didn't appear as if they wanted anything but us out. I mean you could understand this, but we were led to believe that this wouldn't be so, that they would be ready to talk terms with us, sort of thing, in which to help us out. But the barrister just stood up apparently and said, immediate possession and that was that. But as it was, the judge was quite a nice one, and he asked my husband about, you know, if he could pay the arrears, and if he couldn't pay if he was prepared to make some proposal, which is what we did.

So this was accepted? Yes, this was accepted.

And has it worked pretty well since? It did, until about August, and then because of lack of work, my husband had to give up his self-employment and take a new job. And really we slipped right back again, and now we're back again in touch with the FWA, that is, we're trying to work something out again.

Now, did the FWA man go with you to court? No.

Now, anything else that he did, or suggested, or sort of arranged? . . . Not really, I don't think. At the case meeting that they had about the whole thing they came to an arrangement where the children could be given free school meals, which is another thing which they weren't having and apparently they're entitled to. And they were given free meals, and the oldest child was going on their school journey, and we couldn't afford to pay the amount, so therefore he had a reduced rate, so he went I think instead of for 12 gns. he went for 3 gns., and that I think was really all they did. The main difficulty was the rent, which is what we wanted the help over.

And do you consider that they really did help you over the rent? Well, it wasn't practical help, I mean, they didn't pay any arrears for us, or offer us any money to pay the arrears. The only thing really which they gave was they arranged this meeting between the different people concerned, but apparently this is something which is done anyway, you know. Had we said to the different people like the Care Committee Officer or the gentleman from WCC, had we explained to them that we wanted this meeting, then we could have had this anyway without going to the FWA.

But you wouldn't have been likely to have known about this, would you? No, that's what I mean, you see. But again it's just one of those things. All this could have been done, but of all the people that were involved, not one person said that this was possible, you see. And the man from the FWA found out about that, and then mostly it was advice. I mean, he was helpful in that way, he suggested we write to various people, like we had this on HP and several other things, and we did write a letter explaining to them what happened, and because of our financial difficulties, we had had to get in touch with a FWA (we didn't say which one), and they had suggested that we make small payments which will be more regular, instead of the larger ones which will be far between, you know.

And did they accept this? Yes, pretty well accepted the thing, and as I say it worked very well until August, and then we sort of got into the same sort of trouble again. But this time, instead of staying self-employed, he didn't; he changed his job completely, and he's now working for an employer which is better for us. For now we know that we're going to get a regular wage every week, more or less.

When the FWA worker was coming to see you, did you understand what he was getting at, when he suggested things, and advised you, and did you understand what he said? Yes, as regards the advice concerning the payment of bills and other debts, yes we did. The only thing is, he seemed to have an obsession about feelings. Everything that arose, or every statement that we made, it was always, well, what were your feelings about this, what were your feelings about this at the time. What do you feel about this situation, or how do you feel about this house, what are your feelings about the house, and that I couldn't understand, because I didn't think that it was helping us in any way.

Why do you think he was like this? I don't know, as I say, I couldn't understand what it had to do with the case. I mean, he knew about our background and we could speak quite freely to him, I mean, like as personal matters about our marriage—you know, whether it made any difference between our relationship as regards the operation I'd had, did we feel any different about it. Did it make any difference to our sex life and all that. I mean, we were quite open, but I just couldn't understand why all the time he'd asked about these feelings.

Did you ever mention it to him? No, we didn't really like to, because he was such a nice person.

Now, why did you feel you couldn't say it to him, you know, why are you talking about this? I think once when he broached on the subject, my husband asked him, you know why, but again, it was an entirely different answer. It didn't really make much difference to the question we'd asked, we still didn't know.

You didn't get an answer? No, no. He got annoyed. Yes, because he said he was supposed to ask the questions, not we ask him. That's right, he comes in to ask questions, and we mustn't ask him questions.

Well, what did you think of this? I don't know. We thought that we'd been put in our place. It was his job after all, he was coming to ask us, we weren't supposed to interrogate him, you know, when he came here. Well, he was very nice, he wasn't at all, you know, put out, or anything like that, he didn't upset us in any way, but he appeared not very pleased with the fact that we'd asked him. This went on for quite a while before eventually we asked him.

Did you feel you had to behave in any special way with him? No, he was a serious, terribly serious, person.

You didn't ever joke with him? No, I think the first time we joked with him was the last time he came, and he came and said to us that he didn't think we needed to call him any more, and he seemed as if to let himself go a little, you know, He was always very pleasant, very nice when he came, you could never find fault with the way he behaved, but we're not sort of terribly serious either of us, but we do find certain things rather amusing, and he didn't appear to find such things . . .

So he wasn't amused. . . . . No, no, we would say something that we thought was funny, and both of us would laugh . . . so that was the end of that, we thought we won't do that any more. Perhaps, I thought that was his job, you know . . .

That he took it very seriously? Yes, you mustn't go down and treat things light-heartedly, and he obviously did take his job seriously, sort of thing. He mustn't do such things, that's the impression we got, you must keep yourself in reserve.

This is a bit of a hard question, but what do you think he thought of you? I don't really know. I think just another case. I mean, he never gave us any idea how he was feeling, whether he liked us. Oh, he did say once that he found us likeable, I believe, we were both very likeable people, I think. But he didn't state whether he liked us.

What do you think that meant? No, I think he included another part of, he was saying that it was a sort of question and answer, he'd ask us why, you know, the house is always full, which it is, we've always got somebody or other visiting, you know, and he said, did we think that we're young and fairly likeable, that everybody's always coming to see us, sort of thing. I think that's what it was. He gave us the impression that he thought so as well. He didn't really say outright. He gave us the impression that that's what his feelings were, I think.

Now, do you think he really understood your problem? Yes and no. I think mainly the sole question was this problem of rent, you know, and really the only help we really needed was financial, which is obvious. But he did give us a different outlook on things. I mean, we'd had so much trouble with it, that we really had given up hope, you know, we were really down and all that. And myself, I really couldn't see any way of getting out of it, you know, until he came along. If he hadn't came along, I don't know really what would have happened, but when he did come he sort of gave us a new light, and it bucks me up a bit. I managed to get a few things done which I wouldn't have been able to do by myself, which is quite definite, you know. But I've forgotten the question now.

Well, do you really think he understood your problems, and you said 'yes' and 'no'. Yes and no. You see, he looked at my problem, and my problem was money, but he considered my problem was me, you know, it was me, I wouldn't be bothered. Because he came to the conclusion that with help, you know, with his backing, I could do these things, which I did, you know. But without him I would have been lost, which at the time I was completely, you know. I think really he did understand the problem, whereas at the time I didn't think he did.

So, looking back on it, you think he probably saw a bit more to it than you did in fact? Yes. As an outsider, he had more experience what it was. Well, actually I told him, you know, I didn't know what to do, I was at a complete loss.

And what you felt at the time was the rent plus the . . . Yes.

But he thought it was a bit more than that? Exactly. Well it was everything, which it was, but it wasn't only that, there were several other things, you know. And then, of course, to top it all, I did ask him if he could lend us some money, I forget how much it was, £30 I think. To pay the electric light. That's right, yes, and he agreed. You see, he said I have to go away and have a meeting, and we have to go through all sorts of different things to get this money. So I agreed. Well, as soon as I'd asked him I thought well it's not going to be right that I should ask him for money, so I went and asked the fellow I was working with and of course straight away he wrote me out a cheque, you know, and I paid him back within a matter of weeks, you know. So of course when he came the next time, I said, I'm ever so sorry, I've got the money, you know. So he was pleased at the fact that I'd done it on my own, but again he was annoyed because he'd 'gone to so much trouble, you know to do this. But it was just the fact of asking him, and knowing that he was going to give me the money, it sort of butted me up, and I got some on my own, you know. I've done the selfsame thing, but I don't know, it just seemed wrong to accept money from him.

Do you think on the whole he did the right thing? Do you think he handled things in the right way? Really yes. I think he did the best he could.

Only if you'd been in his position do you think you would have done anything different? I don't think so, I think he did what he could at the time, really, I don't think he could have done any more. Yes, I think he did the best he could, you know, with the problem concerned.

Some of the people we've talked to felt they were helped by going to the FWA, others felt it really hadn't made much difference? Now do you think it made any difference to you? Well, we sat down and thought about it afterwards, and we found that everything that had happened really we could have done on our own. And most of it we had done on our own.

Suppose you knew someone fairly well who had problems like yours, would you suggest they went to the FWA? Depends what their problems are.

Yes, but I mean, in your situation. Yes.

You know, financial problems. I would, yes. Because we've benefited if only from the advice. I mean, even to have someone to talk to, tell someone, especially someone like him, because as I said he was so terribly sympathetic. Even financial though they help, it's just the fact that we didn't ask for money.

You think that if you'd really asked for money, you would have got it? Yes, I do. Really, we tried to work it out without asking for money, that's what it all boiled down to. And tried to get round it without borrowing a large sum of money, which we did.

During the period you were going to the FWA, did members of your family know about it, did they know you were going? No.

Any special reason? Did you deliberately not tell them? No, we didn't because the whole idea of the FWA is the trouble we were in and we didn't discuss as I said before, we're not one to discuss . . .

Would you have minded if they'd found out? No, only the fact if they found out, they may have found out about the rent or anything else, and I wouldn't have liked that very much. A social disgrace for some reason, God only knows why, I mean, there's no crime, really, in being in debt, but probably because it was our fault and we do tend to always hear of people who say, you've done it all, well it's your fault, that's what they would say about us!

So in a way you didn't tell them because you mentioned earlier that you didn't want your parents to feel obliged to help you? Yes.

And also you felt that it was perhaps some shame to you if they did find out about it? Yes, it would, I would have felt some sort of shame.

You expected them to be critical? Yes. The mere fact that we've got a lot of children, that's why, you know. I mean, usually you find families with children, well they are aren't they . . . with a lot of children. You see a woman with six children, and straight away the vision comes into your mind of some wife, walking round with an old mac on, which is true.

Do you have this feeling from your family anyway, from your parents? Do you think they're slightly disapproving of the fact that you've got a lot of children? No, well, they can't really. Mum had seven. But I don't think they mind, I mean, it doesn't make much difference, I think. In fact they're really quite envious, although we're already the family paupers. We're the poor ones who haven't got their own house, you see.

Have you ever told them since that you've been? No.

Did you ever discuss such things? No, I mean we know of other difficulties that the rest of the family have been in. No doubt they know some of those that we've been in. But we've never discussed it with them ourselves. We've never discussed with the person who's in trouble themselves.

A sort of tactful silence. It is really. . . . I mean we help each other out. But if my brother-in-law was to come down and ask for help now, it's possible that we'd give it to him, but it's not the sort of thing we do, to go and tell all the other brothers and sisters, that such a thing had happened. And vice versa, they'd be the same, it's just one of those things.

What about your friend? Did you ever discuss it with her? No, because although I've been friendly with her for quite a few years now, about three, at the time she wasn't living here when it was really bad, you know, sort of thing. She is the sort of person I could discuss it with for I know it wouldn't go any further, but it just isn't me. I just don't talk about such things to anybody else.

Now, how did things stand at your last interview with your worker? You said he kind of relaxed a bit the last time you saw him. He did. He became a different man all of a sudden.

But he was the one who suggested he shouldn't come any more, is that right? Yes, it was him.

What did you think, did you agree? Yes. We agreed, yes, because we'd felt like that for quite a while.

You'd talked about it? Yes, but we didn't really like to say to him, well we don't need your help any more, because it seemed as if we'd used him, got what we could, and then was going to dispense with him like that, and we didn't want to. . . . Like a relationship.

You thought you might hurt his feelings? No, not hurt his feelings, so much as he'd be given the wrong impression of us. He may think, well that's it, then, and that's all they wanted, and they've got that. As long as he was willing to come and see us, then we were willing to see him. Although we didn't agree that it was necessary any more but we didn't like to tell him, you know, that we no longer need your services, because I felt that it was ingratitude, you know, as if we weren't grateful for what he'd done, and that was it, we'd used him, and weren't interested any more. And this wasn't so, because we were grateful and as I said, as long as he considered it necessary, we were quite willing to go along with it.

But you were quite pleased when he thought that it was time to stop? Yes, we were, really. Yes, he joked as well, quite a bit himself. And it was then I think that we said, because he asked a question, I can't remember what the question was, but it was then we said that we thought that the questions he asked was as if, you know, we were having trouble with our marriage. The first time he came, you'd think that I was going to leave my husband or he was going to leave me, that was the impression we got, you know what I mean.

That he was behaving as though you were about to split up? Exactly.

That he was to try and keep you together? Exactly.

Whereas this wasn't the problem at all? No, it wasn't the problem at all, you know. And that was the impression we got. And we told him this, at the last visit. To be truthful, I can't really remember what his answer was, but I know we told him and he wasn't annoyed, he took it in quite good form. There again, he was in a very good mood, you know, at the time.

So you both agreed it was time to stop? Perhaps you thought you could have stopped a good deal earlier? Yes. Not a good deal, he only used to come once a week, but for about a month before we'd been ready . . .

Now I'd like to ask you one final question. The FWA is anxious to help people with problems like yours. Could you think of any way in which they could do it better? Can you think of any improvement in the kind of service that you had? Well, not really, because I don't know to what extent they can go, you know, to help people. I think they do their best, which is what our worker did. No, well, I think they do what they can, as regards helping you.

Was there any aspect in which you were disappointed, you thought there was anything he'd missed out, or anything . . .? You mentioned this business about the court. We were disappointed in that.

Things were not as you'd expected or had been led to believe. I don't think that was his fault. No I don't think it was his fault. That's the agreement they came to at the case meeting, but apparently it wasn't carried any further, and in that case he'd done all he could. I mean, he weren't there. No, that's entirely out of his jurisdiction, sort of thing. I mean, he done what he could sort of thing, and gone as far as he could, and he was under the impression as we were, that this was done, and when we told him he was quite astounded as well, because he was under the same impression that this was going to be talked over and arranged at the court hearing, which it wasn't. I mean, we were both under the same impression, that was nothing to do with him. And as I say, I think they help in the best way that they can, and we weren't disappointed, not really. He did what he could, sort of thing, and when we did ask for money, which was for the debt, he was quite prepared, although he didn't promise anything, but he said if he could get it, he would, and as it so happened, when he did come and see us again, he had made arrangements to get this money. He said he couldn't get it that day, that it would take some time, but I think he did the best he could with what he had, the best sort of thing, and the only disappointment wasn't anything to do with him, but the court. I think he did a good job.

How do you feel, looking back on it, about going to this Association for help? You mentioned that you waited a long time, and wanted very much to work things out yourselves. Looking back, do you think it was the right thing to do, that you went to them? Yes. Definitely. And I wish we had known sooner, because I think things wouldn't have got so bad as what they had, if we had gone there sooner.

You see, some people that we've talked to felt that going to something like the FWA, people feel that they're cadging or . . . They do, we did.

Did you feel this, was this something that you felt in yourselves, or that you were made to feel because of the way he behaved? No, he didn't make us feel like that.

This was just the feeling you had about yourselves? It's the feeling that anybody would get, it's just a natural feeling, that you've been cadging. Especially when it happens, like to us, twice. The first time we were badly in trouble, and somebody comes to help you. Then when it happens again, it makes you feel terrible, doesn't it? The fellow comes, and does all he can to get you out of it, sort of thing, and then for no reason at all you drop back straight into it. If it was to happen two or three times, I should imagine you really would feel bad. It definitely did make us feel like cadging, as if we were cadging. Although you're only cadging help.

Notes

Notes to chapter 1

1 J. McVicker Hunt, 'On the Judgement of Social Workers as a Source of Information in Social Work Research', in *Use of Judgements as Data in Social Work Research* (New York: National Association of Social Workers, 1959), p. 38; Fred Massarik, 'The Survey Method in Social Work: Past, Present, and Potential', in *Survey Research in the Social Sciences*, ed. by Charles Y. Glock (New York: Russell Sage Foundation, 1967), pp. 377–422; Ann W. Shyne, 'Casework Research: Past and Present', *Social Casework*, vol. 43 (November 1962), pp. 467–73.

2 For some recent exceptions to this generalization, see Richard Pomeroy, Harold Yahr, and Lawrence Podell, *Studies in Public Welfare: Reactions of Welfare Clients to Caseworker Contact* and *Studies in Public Welfare: Reactions of Welfare Clients to Social Service* (The Centre for the Study of Urban Problems, The City University of New York); William J. Reid and Ann W. Shyne, *Brief and Extended Casework* (New York: Columbia University Press, 1969); Joel G. Sacks, Panke M. Bradley, and Dorothy Fahs Beck, *Clients' Progress Within Five Interviews* (New York: Family Service Association of America, 1970); Phyllis R. Silverman, *The Client Who Drops Out: A Study of Spoiled Helping Relationships*, unpublished Ph.D. dissertation, Florence Heller Graduate School for Advanced Studies in Social Welfare, Brandeis University, 1968. An example of the more usual approach can be found in H. Gottesfeld's study, 'Professionals and Delinquents Evaluate Professional Methods with Delinquents', *Social Problems* (summer 1965), vol. 13. In an interesting footnote the author states, 'The professionals originated the questionnaire items; had the delinquents originated the questionnaire items, new dimensions may have been present. Thus, there may be preferences of the delinquent which were not expressed through the research instrument,' p. 57.

3 See, for example, Robert G. Ballard and Emily H. Mudd, 'Some Sources of Differences between Client and Agency Evaluation of Effectiveness of Counselling', *Social Casework*, vol. 39, No. 1 (1958), pp. 30–5; Leonard S.

Kogan, 'The Short-Term Case in a Family Agency', *Social Casework*, vol. 38, Nos. 5, 6, 7 (1957), pp. 231–8, 296–302, 366–74; Leonard S. Kogan, J. McVicker Hunt, and Phyllis F. Bartelme, *A Follow-up Study of the Results of Social Casework* (New York: Family Service Association of America, 1953); Sacks, Bradley and Beck, op. cit.

4   See, for example, Francis A. Board, 'Patients' and Physicians' Judgements of Outcome of Psychotherapy in an Outpatient Clinic', *AMA Archives of General Psychiatry*, vol. 1 (1959), pp. 185–96; Marcia Kraft Goin, Joe Yamamoto, and Jerome Silverman, 'Therapy Congruent with Class-Linked Expectations', *AMA Archives of General Psychiatry*, vol. 13 (1965), pp. 133–7; Carl R. Rogers, 'Changes in the Maturity of Behaviour as Related to Therapy', in Carl R. Rogers and Rosalind F. Dymond (eds.), *Psychotherapy and Personality Change* (Chicago: University of Chicago Press, 1954), pp. 215–37; Helen H. Avnet, 'How Effective is Short-Term Therapy?', in Lewis R. Wolberg, *Short-Term Psychotherapy* (New York: Grune and Stratton, 1965), pp. 7–22.

5   Dorothy Fahs Beck, 'Potential Approaches to Research in the Family Service Field', *Social Casework*, vol. 40 (July 1959), p. 390.

6   'Crisis Discerned for Social Work', *New York Times*, May 27, 1968.

7   Adrian Sinfield, *Which Way for Social Work* (London: Fabian Society, May 1969) p. 5.

8   Barbara N. Rodgers and Julia Dixon, *Portrait of Social Work* (Oxford University Press, 1960).

9   Barbara Wootton, 'The Image of the Social Worker', *British Journal of Sociology* (1960), p. 382.

10   Jerome D. Frank, 'Problems of Controls in Psychotherapy as Exemplified by the Psychotherapy Research Project of the Phipps Psychiatric Clinic', in *Research in Psychotherapy*, vol. 1, ed. by Eli A. Rubinstein and Morris B. Parloff (Washington, D.C.: American Psychological Association, 1959), p. 10. A more differentiated version of the same question is provided by Ford and Urban (who paraphrase the views of Ray Hyman and Louis Berger): 'Which set of procedures is effective for what set of purposes when applied to what kinds of patients with which sets of problems and practised by which sort of therapists?' Donald H. Ford and Hugh B. Urban, 'Psychotherapy', *Annual Review of Psychology*, ed. Paul R. Farnsworth (Palo Alto, California: Annual Reviews. Inc. 1967).

11   A partial review of such studies can be found in Hans J. Eysenck, 'The Effects of Psychotherapy', *International Journal of Psychiatry*, vol. 1 (January 1965), pp. 99–142; David Wallace and Jesse Smith, *The Chemung County Research Demonstration with Dependent Multi-Problem Families* (New York: State Charities Aid Association, 1965).

12   Lawrence S. Kubie, reply to Eysenck, 'The Effects of Psychotherapy', op. cit, p. 176.

13   Ray Hyman and Louis Berger, reply to Eysenck, 'The Effects of Psychotherapy', *International Journal of Psychiatry*, vol. 1 (April 1965), pp. 317–18.

14   Jerome D. Frank, *Persuasion and Healing* (New York: Schocken Books, 1963) pp. 13–14.

15   Edwin J. Thomas, 'Selected Socio-behavioural Techniques and

Principles: An Approach to Interpersonal Helping', *Social Work*, vol. 13 (January 1968), p. 12.

16 Allen E. Bergin, 'Some Implications of Psychotherapy Research for Therapeutic Practice', *Journal of Abnormal Psychology*, vol. 71, No. 4 (1966), pp. 235, 237.

17 S. M. Miller and Frank Riessman, *Social Class and Social Policy* (New York: Basic Books, Inc., 1968), Chap. 12; Seymour R. Kaplan, 'Psychotherapeutic Approaches in Working with the Disadvantaged', in *Innovations in Psychotherapy*, ed. G. Goldman and D. Millman (Springfield, Ill.: Charles C. Thomas, in press).

18 William E. Mitchell, 'Amicatherapy: Theoretical Perspectives and an Example of Practice', *Community Mental Health Journal*, vol. 2 (1966), pp. 307–14.

19 Bernard B. Guerney, 'Filial Therapy: Description and Rationale', *Journal of Consulting Psychology*, vol. 28 (1964), pp. 304–10.

20 Charles Hersch, 'The Discontent Explosion in Mental Health', *American Psychologist*, vol. 23 (July 1968), pp. 497–506.

21 In addition to the studies noted in footnote 2, see the following: Hope J. Leichter and William E. Mitchell, *Kinship and Casework* (New York: Russell Sage Foundation, 1967); Alice Overton, 'Taking Help from our Clients', *Social Work*, vol. 5 (April 1960), pp. 42–50; Robert W. Roberts, Kermit T. Wiltse and Barbara B. Griswold, 'Unmarried Mothers' Perceptions of the AFDC Experience', in *Mandate for Research* (Chicago: American Public Welfare Association, 1965), pp. 36–46.

22 Graham B. Blaine, Jr. and Charles C. McArthur, 'What Happened in Therapy as Seen by the Patient and His Psychiatrist', *Journal of Nervous and Mental Disease*, vol. 127 (October 1958), pp. 344–50; Herman Feifel and Janet Eells, 'Patients and Therapists Assess the Same Psychotherapy', *Journal of Consulting Psychology*, vol. 27, No. 4 (1963), pp. 310–18; Isadore Kamin and Jeanne Caughlan, 'Subjective Experiences of Outpatient Psychotherapy', *American Journal of Psychotherapy*, vol. 17 (1963), pp. 660–8; Stanley Lipkin, 'The Client Evaluates Nondirective Psychotherapy', *Journal of Consulting Psychology*, vol. 12 (May-June 1948), pp. 137–46; Stanley Lipkin, 'Clients' Feelings and Attitudes in Relation to the Outcome of Client-Centred Therapy', *Psychological Monographs: General and Applied*, vol. 68, No. 1 (1954), pp. 1–30; Carl R. Rogers and Rosalind F. Dymond (eds.) *Psychotherapy and Personality Change* (Chicago: University of Chicago Press, 1954); Hans H. Strupp, Martin S. Wallach and Michael Wogan, 'Psychotherapy Experience in Retrospect: Questionnaire Survey of Former Patients and Their Therapists', *Psychological Monographs: General and Applied*, vol. 78, No. 11 (1964), pp. 1–45; Hans H. Strupp, Ronald E. Fox and Ken Lessler, *Patients View Their Psychotherapy* (Baltimore: The Johns Hopkins Press, 1969); J. F. Wilder and M. Donald Coleman, 'The "Walk-In" Psychiatric Clinic: Some Observations and Follow-Up', *International Journal of Social Psychiatry*, vol. 9, No. 3, 1963.

23 Hans H. Strupp and Allen E. Bergin, 'Some Empirical and Conceptual Bases for Co-ordinated Research in Psychotherapy: A Critical Review of Issues, Trends and Evidence', *International Journal of Psychiatry*, vol. 7 (February 1969), p. 21.

NOTES TO PAGES 8–14

24 *Research in Psychotherapy*, vol. 1, ed. by Eli A. Rubinstein and Morris B. Parloff (Washington, D.C.: American Psychological Association, 1959); vol. 2, ed. by Hans H. Strupp and Lester Luborsky, 1962; vol. 3, ed. by Shlien, Hunt, Matarazzo and Savage, 1968.

25 *Kinship and Casework*, op. cit.

26 Ibid, p. 205 (italics added).

27 Ibid, p. 205 (italics added).

28 David Rosenthal, 'Changes in Some Moral Values Following Psychotherapy', *Journal of Consulting Psychology*, vol. 19, No. 6 (1955), p. 436.

29 The dangers of 'premature closure' have occasionally been noted by others. See for example, Joseph H. Handlon, reply to Eysenck, 'The effects of Psychotherapy', *International Journal of Psychiatry*, vol. 1 (January 1965), pp. 169–71; Elizabeth Herzog, *Some Guide Lines for Evaluative Research* (Washington, D.C.: U.S. Department of Health, Education and Welfare, 1959).

30 Strupp and Bergin, op. cit., p. 28. See also Charles B. Truax and Robert R. Carkhuff, *Toward Effective Counselling and Psychotherapy* (Chicago: Aldine, 1967).

31 Scott Briar, 'Family Services', in *Five Fields of Social Service: Reviews of Research*, ed. by Henry S. Maas (New York: National Association of Social Workers, 1966), pp. 25, 26.

32 Strupp and Bergin, op. cit., p. 50.

33 Lester H. Gleidman *et al.*, 'Incentives for Treatment Related to Remaining or Improving in Psychotherapy', *American Journal of Psychotherapy*, vol. 11 (July 1957), p. 597.

34 Irvin D. Yalom, 'A Study of Group Therapy Dropouts', *Archives of General Psychiatry*, vol. 14 (April 1966), p. 402.

35 Sacks, Bradley and Beck, op. cit., p. 103.

36 John and Elizabeth Newson, *Four Years Old in an Urban Community*, (Chicago: Aldine, 1968), p. 19.

37 Allen H. Barton and Paul F. Lazarsfeld, 'Some Functions of Qualitative Analysis in Social Research', Reprint No. 181, Bureau of Applied Social Research, Columbia University, New York, p. 345.

38 William I. Thomas and Florian Znaniecki, *The Polish Peasant in Europe and America*, 1st ed., 5 vols, 1918–21.

39 Clifford Shaw, *The Jack-Roller: A Delinquent Boy's Own Story* (Chicago: University of Chicago Press, 1930).

40 Robert K. Merton, *Mass Persuasion: The Social Psychology of a War Bond Drive* (New York: Harper, 1946).

41 Donald R. Cressey, *Other People's Money* (New York: The Free Press, 1953).

42 Fred Davis, *Passage Through Crisis* (Indianapolis: Bobbs-Merrill, 1963).

43 James T. Carey, *The College Drug Scene* (Englewood Cliffs, N.J.: Prentice-Hall, 1968).

44 Peter Lomas, *The Predicament of the Family—A Psychoanalytic Symposium* (Hogarth Press, 1967), p. 12.

45 A recent survey of 213 psychiatric social workers, in the Chicago Metropolitan Community, suggests the continued dominance of psychoanalytic thinking. When asked to report their 'major therapeutic orienta-

tion', the following results were obtained: 66 per cent indicated psychoanalytic; 25 per cent social-community; and 9 per cent for the five remaining orientations. (Based on 200 cases.) The percentage of other mental
health personnel reporting a 'psychoanalytic' orientation was as follows:
89 per cent of the psychoanalysts, 50 per cent of the psychiatrists, and 34
per cent of the clinical psychologists. William E. Henry, John H. Sims, and
S. Lee Spray, 'Mental Health Professionals in Chicago', in *Research in
Psychotherapy*, vol. 3, ed. by John M. Shlien *et al.* (Washington D.C.:
American Psychological Association, Inc., 1968), p. 564.

46   Ernest Greenwood, 'Attributes of a Profession', in *Professionalisation*,
ed. by Howard M. Vollmer and Donald L. Mills (Englewood Cliffs, N.J.:
Prentice-Hall, 1966), p. 12. Similar observations have been made by others:
'Part of the process of professionalizing, in medicine as in other professions,
is to prove to the lay world that the work done is of such a nature that the
client is no judge either of what he needs or what he gets.' Arnold I. Kisch
and Leo G. Reeder, 'Client Evaluation of Physician Performance', *Journal
of Health and Social Behaviour*, vol. 10 (March 1969), p. 52.

47   For a thoughtful discussion of the difficulties encountered by British
social workers in their efforts to become professionalized, see Brian J.
Heraud, *Sociology and Social Work: Perspectives and Problems* (to be published
by Pergamon Press in 1970), Chap. 9.

48   Cf. Norman M. Bradburn and David Caplovitz, *Reports on Happiness*
(Chicago: Aldine, 1965), pp. 5–7; James A. Davis, *Education for Positive
Mental Health* (Chicago: Aldine, 1965), Chap. 2; Norman M. Bradburn,
The Structure of Psychological Well-Being (Chicago: Aldine, 1969), Chap. 3.

49   Lloyd E. Ohlin and William C. Lawrence, 'Social Interaction Among
Clients as a Treatment Problem', *Social Work*, vol. 4 (April 1959), pp. 3–13.

50   Robert Holman, 'Client Power', *New Society*, October 31, 1968, p. 645.

51   'The Deepening Welfare Crisis', *New York Times*, August 1, 1968;
'Welfare Clients Renew Protests', *New York Times*, December 6, 1968.

52   An indication that exploratory studies have low status in psychotherapy research circles *as well* is provided by Levinson's remarks concerning their 'unpublishability'. After noting that researchers rarely undertake
studies 'with the aim of deriving variables for further study', he adds:
'One reason we don't do it, I think, is that it is very hard to get it published.
It just does not fit the model of the usual journal article. You are supposed
to end up with conclusions about the way in which a variable operates
rather than simply saying on the basis of a lot of qualitative observations, "I
propose that this is an important variable; it is as far as I have gotten so
far in my research, but it is still worth publishing on the basis of findings to
date".' Daniel J. Levinson, from a discussion in *Research in Psychotherapy*,
vol. 2, op. cit., pp. 297, 298.

53   For a discussion of the processes leading to the cumulation of scientific
knowledge, with particular reference to the interplay between theory and
research, see Robert K. Merton, *Social Theory and Social Structure*, revised
and enlarged edition (New York: The Free Press, 1957), esp. Chaps. 2
and 3.

54   Ernest Greenwood, 'Social Work Research: A Decade of Re-appraisal',
The Social Service Review, vol. 31 (September 1957), p. 54.

Notes to chapter 2

1   Fred Massarik, 'The Survey Method in Social Work: Past, Present and Potential', op. cit., p. 392.

2   Edgar F. Borgatta, David Fanshel, and Henry J. Meyer, *Social Workers' Perceptions of Clients* (New York: Russell Sage Foundation, 1960), p. 62.

3   All these workers had a university education (a two-year course leading to a diploma in social studies or a three-year course leading to a degree) followed by a professional course in social work, usually of a year's duration.

4   Satisfied 'dropouts' gave the following reasons for not returning. In some instances they felt, unlike their social worker, that they had been helped as much as they possibly could be. In other instances, their original worker had left the agency and they were reluctant to transfer to a new one. On still other occasions they felt they had 'talked themselves out', although they planned to return as soon as they had something new or worthwhile to discuss. Finally, some discontinued in treatment because their spouse refused either to enter or to continue in treatment.

5   The category, 'working class', is admittedly very broad and contains a number of distinctive sub-groupings—a fact that is being increasingly recognized by sociologists and others. (Albert K. Cohen and Harold M. Hodges, Jr., 'Characteristics of the Lower-Blue-Collar-Class', *Social Problems*, vol. 10 (Spring 1963), pp. 303–34.) Within a more differentiated framework, our own respondents might, on the whole, be seen appropriately as 'respectable' working-class, or within terms of American sociology as 'upper lowers'. However, in a preliminary study such as ours such refinements can temporarily be put aside on the grounds that there are meaningful and significant differences between those of 'working-class' and those of 'middle-class' background, and that these merit prior consideration. Thus, throughout the study we shall refer to 'working-class' people and to 'working-class behaviour' recognizing that this first approximation will at a later stage require correction in terms of finer categories.

6   The importance of foresight in qualitative interviewing is stressed by Robert K. Merton, Marjorie Fiske, and Patricia L. Kendall in their discussion of the focused interview, *The Focused Interview* (New York: The Free Press, 1956), pp. 17, 18.

7   The mechanisms which enable everyday conversations to proceed smoothly are perceptively described by Erving Goffman, *The Presentation of Self in Everyday Life* (New York: Doubleday Anchor Books, 1959).

Notes to chapter 3

1   Earlier efforts to develop and work with these ideas can be found in John E. Mayer and Aaron Rosenblatt, 'The Client's Social Context: Its Effect on Continuance in Treatment', *Social Casework*, vol. 45 (November 1964), pp. 511–18 and Rosenblatt and Mayer, 'Client Disengagement and Alternative Treatment Resources', *Social Casework*, vol. 47, (January 1966), pp. 3–12.

2   The best source material is contained in Gerald Gurin, Joseph Veroff, and Shelia Feld, *Americans View Their Mental Health* (New York: Basic Books, 1960).

3   Ibid., pp. 364–7. It should be added that a great many people chose neither alternative; for example, some did nothing, others resorted to prayer.

4   Gurin, Veroff, and Feld, op. cit.; Charles Kadushin, *Why People Go To Psychiatrists* (New York: Atherton, 1969).

5   Studies of working-class families consistently reveal greater closeness to relatives than friends, e.g., Mirra Komarovsky, *Blue-Collar Marriage* (New York: Random House, 1962), John E. Mayer 'Disclosing Marital Problems', *Social Casework*, vol. 48 (June 1967), pp. 342–51.

6   *Other People's Marital Problems* (New York: Community Service Society, 1966). For other studies indicating a lack of trust on the part of working-class people, see Albert K. Cohen and Harold M. Hodges, Jr., 'Characteristics of the Lower-Blue-Collar-Class', *Social Problems*, vol. 10 (Spring 1963), p. 323; Herbert J. Gans, *The Urban Villagers* (New York: The Free Press, 1962), pp. 236–7.

7   Little is known about the 'confiding' patterns of different groups in the population. For some beginning studies concerned with sex, class and nationality differences, see Sidney Jourard, *The Transparent Self* (Princeton, N.J.: Van Nostrand, 1964); Komarovksy, op. cit.; Mayer, 'Disclosing Marital Problems', op. cit.

8   Kenneth C. W. Kammeyer and Charles D. Bolton, 'Community and Family Factors Related to the Use of a Family Service Agency', *Journal of Marriage and the Family*, vol. 30 (August 1968), pp. 493, 494.

9   Andrew Ferber, Deborah Kligler, Israel Zwerling, and Marilyn Mendelsohn, 'Current Family Structure: Psychiatric Emergencies and Patient Fate', *Archives of General Psychiatry*, vol. 16 (June 1967), p. 667.

Notes to chapter 4

1   Gerald Gurin, Joseph Veroff, and Shelia Feld, *Americans View Their Mental Health* (New York: Basic Books, 1960), Chaps. 9 and 10. In one study, 42 per cent of the persons seeking help from a Neighbourhood Service Centre in the Bronx indicated that either they or someone in their household had had a 'nervous breakdown'; only 11 per cent of their neighbours (who were non-clients) made such a statement. Lucille Nahemow, 'Comparison of Users and Nonusers of a Community Mental Health Facility', *Proceedings*, 76th Annual Convention, APA (1968) pp. 669, 700.

2   Leonard S. Kogan, 'The Utilisation of Social Work Research', *Social Casework*, vol. 44 (December 1963) pp. 569–74.

3   The authors of another study, concerned with clients of a Family Service Agency in California, have recently underscored the vagaries of formal referral agents. 'The interviews suggested that the professional referral sources do little to provide prospective clients with a [clear] understanding of just what to expect from the Agency. Interviews with both clients and doctors indicate that doctors most often recommend the Family Service in much the same way as they do a medical prescription. The patient is simply told that the service would be good for him, and something may be said about fees. School principals and lawyers also appear to impart very little information to clients about what actually goes on in the

services rendered by a Family Service Agency. Similarly, newspaper articles tend to stress the value of the Agency, the qualifications of the Director, the sources of financial support, and something of the fee structure, but almost nothing about what kinds of experiences the client may expect at the Agency.' Charles D. Bolton and Kenneth Kammeyer, 'The Decision to Use a Family Service Agency', *Family Co-ordinator*, vol. 17 (January 1968), p. 52. In a similar connection, Malcolm Ford observes: 'A referrer may not understand the particular agency's function and its methods of work or she may misinterpret these or anticipate what will be done for the client she intends to refer. She may convey—either directly or indirectly— to the client false ideas of what will happen, or give false reassurances. On the other hand she may be so vague that the client does not gain sufficient hope or support to feel confident enough to follow through'. 'Financial Help as a Social Work Technique: Some Emotional and Organisational Problems', *Social Work*, vol. 24 (January 1967), p. 21.

4   There were other processes generating unrealistically high expectations that should be noted, although they have no necessary connection with referral agents *per se*. Several clients took the agency's routine way of operating as an indicator that they in particular were bound to receive material help. One client was convinced that the agency was going to help because they wrote her a letter offering her an appointment. Another expected material assistance because she had received it in the past and was even *more desperate* now. Still another believed the agency 'would do something' because they had made her wait two months for an appointment.

5   See, in this connection, the fruitful conceptualizations worked out by Eliot Freidson (who distinguishes the lay from the professional referral structure), 'Client Control and Medical Practice', *American Journal of Sociology*, vol. 65 (January 1960), pp. 374–82 and *Patients' Views of Medical Practice* (New York: Russell Sage Foundation, 1961). Recent empirical analyses of referral processes can be found in Bolton and Kammeyer, op. cit., pp. 47–53 and Charles Kadushin, *Why People Go to Psychiatrists* (New York: Atherton, 1969). Finally, for an annotated bibliography on 'the career of seeking help', see Eliot Freidson, 'The Sociology of Medicine: A trend report and bibliography', *Current Sociology*, vol. 10/11, No. 3, 1961–2, pp. 159–61.

Notes to chapter 5

1   Charles D. Bolton and Kenneth Kammeyer, 'The Decision to Use a Family Agency', *The Family Co-ordinator*, vol. 17 (January 1968), p. 52. This is, of course, part of the larger problem of the general public's knowledge of and attitude towards social work. A study in Holland of 'What the General Public Knows and Thinks of the Social Services' found that 'Older people and those who belong to a lower social level regard social work *first and foremost* as a form of insurance against emergencies by which anyone may be confronted at a certain moment: problems of which one need not be ashamed, such as illness, difficulties in bringing up one's children and old age. . . . Younger people and persons belonging to a higher social level, on the other hand, regard it as something far removed from themselves.

They think that it is *first and foremost* something for those who are social misfits. . . .' *Some findings of social welfare research sponsored by the Ministry of Cultural Affairs, Recreation and Social Welfare.* A small pilot study by one of the present authors (N.T.) concluded that there was a serious lack of knowledge about social work. See 'The Public and the Social Worker', *Social Work,* vol. 19, No. 1. January 1962.

2 Gerald Sanctuary, *Marriage Under Stress* (London: Allen & Unwin, 1968), pp. 55, 59, 60. See also William J. Reid and Barbara L. Shapiro, 'Client Reaction To Advice', *Social Science Review* vol. 43, No. 2 (June 1969), pp. 165-73.

3 A similar reticence on the part of clients to question their workers clearly emerges from the interviews which Phyllis R. Silverman conducted with seventeen Negro clients and their workers. See 'Intake', unpublished ms., drawn from *The Client Who Drops Out: A Study of Spoiled Helping Relationships,* Ph.D. Dissertation, Florence Heller Graduate School for Advanced Studies in Social Welfare, Brandeis University, 1968.

4 Occasionally, clients gave what can only be a very garbled picture of the worker's interpretations—a further indication that the latter's problem-solving orientation was foreign to them. Mrs Linton, whose husband had died as the result of a fall from a scaffold, remarked: 'Mr Jones [the social worker] kept telling me that my husband's death was more or less my fault. He more or less said that *I* was to blame for it. He never sort of understood that my husband got killed and it was *his* fault. He didn't seem to understand at all.' Myers and Roberts, who studied a small group of psychiatric patients in New Haven, provide a similar instance of a 'derailment' in understanding. They cite the case of a lower-class patient who 'expressed her pleasure with the course of treatment and praised her therapist', but who capped her description of the treatment (which was psychoanalytically oriented) with the following statement:

Dr Heston keeps telling me I'm supposed to forget my past and the terrible things I done. For months now, he's been telling me to forget my troubles. He says not to worry about my problems and put the past out of my mind. That's exactly what I done. I put the past out of my head. I forgot all about it and now I'm happy and lots better.

Jerome K. Myers and Bertram H. Roberts, *Family and Class Dynamics in Mental Illness* (New York: Wiley, 1959), p. 209.

5 For similar findings—specifically, an inability on the part of lower-class patients to understand the 'intent' of their insight-oriented psychiatrists—see Myers and Roberts, op. cit., pp. 207-10.

6 Norman Q. Brill and Hugh A. Storrow, 'Social Class and Psychiatric Treatment', in *Mental Health of the Poor,* ed. by Frank Riessman, Jerome Cohen, and Arthur Pearl (New York: The Free Press, 1964), pp. 68-74: August B. Hollingshead and Fredrick C. Redlich, *Social Class and Mental Illness* (New York: Wiley, 1958); James T. McMahon, 'The Working Class Psychiatric Patient: A Clinical View', in *Mental Health of the Poor,* op. cit., pp. 283-302; Betty Overall and H. Aronson, 'Expectations of Psychotherapy in Patients of Lower Socioeconomic Class', *Mental Health of the Poor,* op. cit., 76-87.

7 *Health, Culture, and Community*, ed. by Benjamin D. Paul (New York: Russell Sage Foundation, 1955), p. 471.

8 John E. Mayer, *The Disclosure of Marital Problems* (New York: The Community Service Society, 1966), abridged in 'Disclosing Marital Problems', *Social Casework*, vol. XLVIII, No. 6 (June 1967), pp. 342–51.

9 Mirra Komarovsky, *Blue-Collar Marriage* (New York: Random House, 1962); Lee Rainwater, Richard P. Coleman, and Gerald Handel, *Working-man's Wife* (New York: Oceana, 1959).

10 For descriptions of working-class culture, see Catherine S. Chilman, *Growing Up Poor*, Washington, D.C.: U.S. Department of Health, Education and Welfare, 1966; Albert K. Cohen and Harold M. Hodges, Jr., 'Characteristics of the Lower-Blue-Collar-Class', *Social Problems*, vol. 10 (Spring 1963), pp. 303–34; Warren C. Haggstrom, 'The Power of the Poor', in *Mental Health of the Poor*, op. cit., pp. 205–23; *Low-Income Life Styles*, ed. by Lola M. Irelan (Washington, D.C.: Department of Health, Education and Welfare, 1966); Walter B. Miller, 'Implications of Urban lower-class Culture for Social Work', *Social Service Review*, vol. 33 (September 1959), pp. 219–36.

11 Seymour Martin Lipset, *Political Man* (Garden City, N.Y.: Anchor Books, 1963), pp. 87–126.

12 Irelan, op. cit.

13 Komarovsky, op. cit., p. 192.

14 Eliot Freidson, *Patients' Views of Medical Practice* (New York: Russell Sage Foundation, 1961), p. 107.

15 In our view, people's theories of causality, even though they remain implicit (and this may typically be the case), importantly affect many of their attitudes, values, beliefs and actions—and thus require more research attention than they have received. In this connection, Florence Hollis points out the bearing that theories of causation have for the social worker's treatment aims: '. . . when we speak of the influence on treatment aims of causation or of modifiability, we actually mean the worker's *thinking about* causation and modifiability. How he views these factors rests not only on his individual perception and judgment, but also upon the body of theory by which his conclusions are influenced. A worker viewing a client and his situation from the vantage point of a different theory might well come to different conclusions about causation and modifiability, and therefore envisage different treatment aims. Theory of causation and treatment goals are closely related.' *Casework: A Psychosocial Therapy* (New York: Random House, 1964), pp. 212, 213.

16 For observations or data bearing on this general point (though not always directly), see Cohen and Hodges, op. cit., pp. 319, 321; Robert Endleman, 'Moral Perspectives of Blue-Collar Workers', in *Blue-Collar World*, ed. by Arthur B. Shostak and William Gomberg (Englewood Cliffs, N.J.: Prentice-Hall 1964), pp. 308–16; Lipset, op. cit., pp. 92, 95; Julian L. Woodward, 'Changing Ideas on Mental Illness and Its Treatment', *American Sociological Review*, vol. 16, No. 4, August 1951, pp. 443–53, esp. p. 445; Bruce P. Dohrenwend and Edwin Chin-Shong, 'Social Status and Attitudes Toward Psychological Disorder: The Problem of Tolerance of Deviance', *American Sociological Review*, vol. 32 (June 1967), pp. 417–33. In

this connection it is worth noting some findings from child-rearing studies. Thus, a recent British study found that middle-class mothers prefer to manage their children through the use of reasoning, tending to treat their children from a very early age as if they were capable of being persuaded by rational argument, whilst working-class mothers are much less likely to embark on lengthy verbal explanation and rely on the exercise of authority. Or in dealing with children's quarrels the middle-class mother tends to emphasize reasoned adjudication and the working-class mother tends to say, 'Go and hit him back'. See 'Some Social Differences in the Process of Child-Rearing', John and Elizabeth Newson in *Penguin Social Sciences Survey* 1968, ed. J. Gould.

17   Certain of the conceptions developed in this chapter were stimulated by the pioneering work of Shirley Star, who has pointed out how differences in beliefs about mental illness can derive from differences in people's underlying and implicit *premises* about the nature of behaviour. 'The Place of Psychiatry in Popular Thinking', paper presented at the annual meeting of the American Association for Public Opinion Research, May 1957. See also, Elaine Cumming and John Cumming, *Closed Ranks—An Experiment in Mental Health Education* (Cambridge, Mass.: Harvard University Press, 1957).

Notes to chapter 6

1   Florence Hollis, *Casework: A Psychosocial Therapy* (New York: Random House, 1964) and 'Explorations in the Development of a Typology of Casework Treatment', *Social Casework*, vol. 48 (June 1967), pp. 335–41.

2   In varying degrees, this was true also of satisfied clients seeking material assistance. Speaking more generally, there is a definite overlap in the processes leading these two types of clients to feel satisfied. But there are also significant differences which accounts for our separate analyses of these cases.

3   These findings are from a NORC-HIF survey cited in Eliot Freidson, *Patients' Views of Medical Practice* (New York: Russell Sage, 1961), p. 80. See also Irving K. Zola, 'Illness Behavior of the Working Class: Implications and Recommendations', in *Blue-Collar World*, ed. Arthur B. Shostak and William Gomberg (Englewood Cliffs, N.J.: Prentice-Hall, 1964), pp. 350–61.

4   Additional case histories documenting the importance of this activity on the part of the worker can be found in Florence Hollis, *Women in Marital Conflict* (New York: Family Service Association of America, 1949), pp. 193, 194.

5   Several of our middle-class clients apparently preferred that the mechanics of the advice-giving process not be overly apparent. One said, approvingly: 'She sort of gave you her advice but in a roundabout way.' Another remarked, 'She gave me her advice more or less the way I wanted to hear it. She didn't sort of agree or disagree.'

6   Nevitt Sanford, 'Discussion of Papers on Measuring Personality Change', in *Research in Psychotherapy*, vol. 2, ed. Hans H. Strupp and Lester Luborsky (Washington, D.C.: American Psychological Association, 1962), p. 156.

7   Elizabeth Herzog, *Some Guide Lines for Evaluative Research* (Washington, D.C.: U.S. Department of Health, Education and Welfare, Social Security Administration, Children's Bureau, 1959), p. 32.

8   For illustrations of how the making of an appointment may be used as a 'threat', see Elvira Hughes Brigg, 'The Application Problem: A Study of Why People Fail to Keep First Appointments', *Social Work*, vol. 10 (April 1965), pp. 71–8.

9   Alvin W. Gouldner, 'Cosmopolitans and Locals: Toward an Analysis of Latent Social Roles—1', Administrative Quarterly, vol. 2 (December 1957), pp. 281–306; Alvin W. Gouldner and Helen P. Gouldner, *Modern Sociology* (New York: Harcourt, Brace, and World, 1963), pp. 387, 388; Eliot Freidson, op. cit., pp. 186–9.

10   August B. Hollingshead and Frederick C. Redlich, *Social Class and Mental Illness: A Community Study* (New York: Wiley, 1958), pp. 267, 268.

11   Florence Hollis, 'A Profile of Early Interviews in Marital Counselling', *Social Casework*, vol. 49 (January 1968), pp. 35–43 and 'Continuance and Discontinuance in Marital Counselling and some Observations on Joint Interviews', *Social Casework*, vol. 49 (March 1968), pp. 167–74; Edward J. Mullen, 'Casework Communication', *Social Casework*, vol. 49 (November 1968), pp. 546–51, 'The Relation between Diagnosis and Treatment in Casework', *Social Casework*, vol. 50 (April 1969), pp. 218–26, 'Differences in Worker Style in Casework', *Social Casework*, vol. 50 (June 1969), pp. 347–53; and William J. Reid, 'Characteristics of Casework Intervention', *Welfare in Review*, vol. 5 (October 1967), pp. 11–19.

12   Gerald Gurin, Joseph Veroff, and Shelia Feld, *Americans View Their Mental Health* (New York: Basic Books, 1960), p. 323.

Notes to chapter 7

1   Helen Harris Perlman, *Social Casework* (Chicago: University of Chicago Press, 1957), pp. 37, 38.

2   Sub-cultural differences within England and the U.S. have yet to be fully explored. Available data suggest that Puerto Ricans and Jewish refugees of Eastern European origin in the U.S., as well as West Indians living in England, consider help-seeking less shameful than native-born persons. See, respectively, Richard Pomeroy, Harold Yahr, and Lawrence Podell, *Studies in Public Welfare: Reactions of Welfare Clients to Social Service* (New York: Centre for the Study of Urban Problems, City University of New York), pp. 11, 12; Ivor Svarc, 'Client Attitudes Toward Financial Assistance: A Cultural Variant', *Social Service Review* (June 1956), pp. 136–46; Katrin FitzHerbert, 'West Indians and the Child Care Service', *New Society* (April 27, 1967), pp. 604–6.

3   Lawrence Podell, *Families on Welfare in New York City* (New York: Centre for the Study of Urban Problems, City University of New York), pp. 31, 32.

4   Ivor Svarc, op. cit. p. 144.

5   Svarc, ibid, p. 141.

6   In the survey just referred to, involving mothers who were receiving public assistance in New York City, 71 per cent agreed with the following

statement: 'A lot of people getting money from welfare don't deserve it.' Podell, op. cit., p. 32.

7 Less than half of the mothers in the Podell study (44 per cent)agreed with the following statement: 'The Department of Welfare has no right to ask questions about how people spend their money.' Ibid., p. 32.

8 Leonard Schatzman and Anselm Strauss, 'Social Class and Modes of Communication', *American Journal of Sociology*, vol. 60 (January 1955), p. 331.

9 It is well recognized that the punitive views outlined in this chapter are shared not only by clients but are variously distributed throughout the middle-class, and, to an unknown extent, throughout the mental health profession itself. See, in this connection, Adrian Sinfield, *Which Way for Social Work?* (London: Fabian Society, May 1969); also the tangential discussion by Hollingshead and Redlich of the 'dislike' which a group of psychiatrists felt towards their lower-class patients, *Social Class and Mental Illness* (New York: Wiley, 1958), pp. 344-51.

Notes to chapter 8

1 The one exception concerns a wife who hoped the agency would provide her with money so that she could get a room apart from her husband. During treatment, however, she decided to remain with her husband, thus removing the need for material help.

2 Richard Pomeroy, Harold Yahr, and Lawrence Podell, *Studies in Public Welfare: Reactions of Clients to Social Service* (New York: Centre for the Study of Urban Problems, City University of New York), p. 73.

3 Elizabeth E. Irvine, 'The Hard-to-Like Family', *Case Conference*, vol. 14 (July 1967), p. 108. A more general discussion of these processes— specifically, the relationship between obligating other people and securing compliance—can be found in Peter M. Blau and W. Richard Scott, *Formal Organisations* (San Francisco: Chandler, 1962), pp. 142, 143, 237.

4 The reader may be interested in a recent survey of 100 clients who received grants from the FWA. The survey is based on an examination of case records, applications for financial help, and talks with the social workers involved; it contains information such as the family composition of the clients, their length of contact with the FWA, and the purpose and amounts of the grants. The average grant, according to the study, was £12 10s., but the range was very wide, extending from £1 10s. to £60. The clients came primarily because they were in debt, especially to the London Electricity Board which was the single biggest creditor (S. Greve, *Financial Help as Part of Social Work*, Family Welfare Association 1968). Some of the strains confronting social workers at the FWA in providing financial help are described by Malcolm Ford. His discussion focuses both on the worker's relationship with the client and, significantly, with the trustees of private funds, 'Financial Help as a Social Work Technique: Some Emotional and Organisational Problems', *Social Work*, op. cit.

Notes to chapter 9

1   This phenomenon whereby mothers coach daughters how to act in the casework situation may be more common than we suspect. Another and even more vivid instance appears in the case of Mrs Norton (a satisfied client in search of interpersonal help):

> The first couple of times that I went to the FWA, I was staying with my mum. But everytime after that I used to go to my mum's because I had left the boy with her and I told mum what I said to the gentleman. And she used to just sit there, saying, 'well that was right' or 'that was wrong'. Or, 'you shouldn't have said that—you should have said this'. If I told the gentleman I used to start an argument with my husband over little things, my mum would say, 'well, you don't always start the argument—John don't give you a chance to finish anything'. Whatever I said wrong, my mum used to put right. And if the subject came up again the next time I went to the FWA, I knew what to say and would tell it the right way. I used to improve myself each time by my mum talking to me. . . . Once I upset mum when I was talking to her, because I said that I told the gentleman that I was a spoiled brat and was niggly. My mum said that was wrong and that I shouldn't have said that. She felt I was making an idiot of myself and it was coming back to me. She thought the gentleman would think I was the cause of all the trouble which I wasn't. So next time I went I put it the right way around. I said, 'when I was small I was spoilt, but I'm not always spoilt now.' I put it round the right way that time, instead of just coming out with it plainly.

2   Martin T. Orne and Paul H. Wender, 'Anticipatory Socialisation for Psychotherapy: Method and Rationale', *American Journal of Psychiatry*, vol. 124 (March 1968), p. 1206.

3   As we noted earlier the workers who were interviewed were told nothing about the earlier interviews that had been conducted with their clients.

4   Erving Goffman, *The Presentation of Self in Everyday Life* (Garden City, New York: Doubleday Anchor, 1959), Chap. 6.

5   Perry Levinson, 'Chronic Dependency: A Conceptual Analysis', *Social Service Review*, vol. 38 (December 1964), p. 376.

6   Peter M. Blau, 'Orientation Toward Clients in a Public Welfare Agency', *Administrative Science Quarterly*, vol. 5 (December 1960), p. 348.

7   There were certain exceptions to this. Mrs Wrighton, a middle-class client whose husband and daughter were also receiving casework treatment, felt aggrieved because, in her opinion, she was receiving less insight into her difficulties than they were: 'I noticed that both Harry and Celia sometimes came back from their hour very elated, and then being terrible angry about it and very upset. And I think that one of the points of going is that you can see something which you haven't been able to see before. But I never had any of this at all with Miss X. I never had the feeling that she'd uncovered something which I didn't know before.'

The role of television is also worth a word at this point. Presumably some people become aware of casework procedures as a result of watching TV depictions of social workers in action. While this was not illustrated by any of the cases we studied, the following excerpt highlights the important role that television may play in other connections. Mrs Stone, who went to the agency to obtain information about obtaining a divorce, was shocked to find that her reactions differed from those observed on TV:

> I seen these people go with problems that you see on telly. You know, a woman might be telling that she's thinking of getting a divorce and that she can't carry on no more. She bursts into tears and you'd be crying there with her. I thought it was strange why I wasn't like that. I was just stone cold, like a brick. I just sat there and said it plain blankly about the divorce. I wasn't upset or nothing, and I thought I *should* have been upset. I was shocked with myself really.

8 Malcolm Ford, 'Financial Help as a Social Work Technique: Some Emotional and Organisational Problems', *Social Work*, op. cit., p. 23.

Notes to chapter 10

1 G. Gurin, J. Veroff, and S. Feld, *Americans View Their Mental Health* (New York: Basic Books, 1960), pp. 304, 305.

2 It is not implied that the particular treatment approaches utilized by different workers was necessarily the result of an articulated philosophy of treatment in which the relative merits of different approaches were explicitly weighed. The selection of treatment approach was probably influenced by the worker's preferred 'style' of working, the particular skills he happened to possess, the traditions and constraints of the setting in which he worked, etc.

3 For a pointed discussion of this and related issues, see Geoffrey Parkinson, 'I Give Them Money', *New Society*, February 5, 1970.

4 Sidney Wasserman, 'The American Social Work Scene: A Biased Viewpoint', *Case Conference*, vol. 15 (March 1969), p. 429. For an excellent discussion of the sources of these shifts in thinking see Charles Hersch, 'The Discontent Explosion in Mental Health', *American Psychologist*, vol. 23 (July 1968), pp. 497–506.

5 Several studies have shown that the gains achieved by 'short-term' therapy are maintained a year or so after the end of treatment. These results, however, do not fully bear on the queries raised above. First, 'short-term' and 'supportive-directive' therapy, while they may have much in common, are not necessarily the same. Secondly, we have in mind longer time spans than have been investigated by the studies undertaken. For a summary of researches investigating the durability of the effects of 'short-term' treatment, see William J. Reid and Ann W. Shyne, *Brief and Extended Casework* (New York: Columbia University Press, 1969), Chap. 8.

6 For example, Rudolf Hoehn-Saric, Jerome D. Frank, Stanley D. Imber, Earl H. Nash, Anthony R. Stone, and Carolyn C. Battle, 'Systematic Preparation of Patients for Psychotherapy—1. Effects on Therapy Behaviour and Outcome', *Journal of Psychiatric Research*, vol. 2, pp. 267–81; Martin T. Orne and Paul H. Wender, 'Anticipatory Socialisation for Psychotherapy: Method and Rationale', *American Journal of Psychiatry*, vol. 124 (March 1968), pp. 1202–12.

7 Elaine Cumming and John Cumming, *Closed Ranks—An Experiment in*

Mental Health Education (Cambridge, Mass.: Harvard University Press, 1957).

8   As a number of observers have pointed out, there is a curious tendency not to perceive, or perhaps not to admit the existence of, cultural differences which are in our midst. Similar differences are, of course, readily discerned (and admitted) when comparisons are made *between* societies. For a discussion of why social workers fail to discern the cultural basis of different social class behaviour see Walter B. Miller, 'Implications of Urban Lower-Class Culture for Social Work', *Social Service Review*, vol. 33 (September 1959), pp. 219–36.

9   For an illuminating discussion of how such considerations tend to be overlooked by individuals in general, see Gustav Ichheiser, 'Misunderstandings in Human Relations', *American Journal of Sociology*, Part 2, vol. 55 (September 1949), entire issue.

10   Kinglsey Davis, *Human Society* (New York: Macmillan, 1949), p. 149.

11   In our view, secondary schools could make a notable contribution if they offered courses in what might be called the sociology of interpersonal relations. These might deal with topics such as the following: the reasons why people act as they do in given situations; the ways in which their behaviour is 'explained' by those with whom they are interacting; the kinds of misunderstandings that arise; the ways in which these spiral into vicious circles and so forth. According to Schofield—who strongly advocates similar instruction—the schools, at least in the U.S., have done very little along the lines indicated. (William Schofield, *Psychotherapy: The Purchase of Friendship* [Englewood Cliffs, N.J.: Prentice-Hall, 1964], p. 155.) Courses of the type suggested might help to prepare working-class people for insight-oriented therapy; but of far greater significance, in our view, they would enable them to cope more effectively with the strains that arise in their lives and perhaps prevent others from occurring. Similar views are expressed by Schofield (Ibid., p. 154): 'With a scientifically psychological orientation toward the understanding both of self and others the individual [as the result of instruction] is less likely to be victimised either by his own emotions or by the irrationalities of others.'

It need hardly be added that the unsophisticated behavioural conceptions of working-class people are in no sense 'natural' to them, so-to-speak, but derive, at least in part, from particular socializing experiences. In the course of growing up, young people of middle-class background are exposed to relevant books and articles; their parents, friends and acquaintances are apt to have sophisticated views about behaviour; they are apt to go on to college and so forth. Working-class people, on the other hand, are unlikely to be exposed to socializing influences of this nature and the school, in our opinion, is a logical place to make up for such disadvantages.

12   Orne and Wender, op. cit.

Notes to Appendix 3

1   The field of professional behaviour has been increasingly studied by sociologists during the last decade, and reveals a good deal of consensus concerning the nature of the norms regulating client-practitioner interaction.

Our own discussion of these norms is drawn primarily from the work of Harold L. Wilensky and Charles N. Lebeaux, *Industrial Society and Social Welfare* (New York: Russell Sage, 1958), pp. 298–303 and Robert K. Merton, 'Some Preliminaries to a Sociology of Medical Education', in *The Student-Physician*, ed. by Merton, Reader, and Kendall (Cambridge, Mass.: Harvard University Press, 1957) p. 74.

2 Wilensky and Lebeaux, op. cit., p. 301.

3 For a brief discussion of how physicians fail to live up to ideal requirements, see David Mechanic, *Medical Sociology* (New York: The Free Press, 1968), pp. 112–14.

4 Wilensky and Lebeaux, op. cit., pp. 299, 300.

5 One of the workers whom we interviewed said, in reference to one of her clients who took part in our study: 'Mrs Watt used to play down the importance of the interviews by calling them "chats" and saying it was nice to get away from the children. . . . Once I said to her that perhaps they were more than that, to which Mrs Watt replied with a slight affirmative and passed on to some other topic.'

6 S. M. Miller and Frank Riessman, 'The Working-Class Subculture: A New View' in *Blue-Collar World* ed. Arthur B. Shostak and William Gomberg (Englewood Cliffs, N.J.: Prentice-Hall, 1964) p. 32.

7 Sociologists have tended to implicitly assume an awareness on the part of clients (working-class or otherwise)—which may or may not be the case. Note, for example, the following discussion of the physician-patient relationship:

> The social role of the physician . . . includes the privilege of confidential access to extraordinary intimacies of his patient's physical and social experience. . . . Moreover, it is a privilege which the doctor expects from his patient just as a doctor expects to be held responsible himself for holding in confidence the knowledge which results from this privilege. Because these are normative patterns of expected behaviour, the doctor does not have to instruct each patient concerning his privileges and obligations as a physician; *his patient has learned about the doctor's social role as part of his general participation in a society and his indoctrination into its culture.*
>
> *Similarly, the patient has learned what his society 'normally expects' from 'a patient'. As he assumes the role of patient, his behaviour is guided accordingly.*
> (Italics added)

Samuel W. Bloom, *The Doctor and His Patient* (New York: Russell Sage, 1963) p. 67.

Index of names